The Off-Wheel Pottery Book

Mother and child from Nayrit, West Mexico. The standing woman, about 16" tall, holds a diminutive baby. Date: 300-900 A.D. There has been some repair and restoration at the neck. PROPERTY OF DR. MICHAEL MCDONALD.

THE OFF-WHEEL POTTERY BOOK

Ida Claire Larden
and
Raymond Hull

Charles Scribner's Sons/New York

Abstract sculpture on page i by Arthur Freeman, 8″ high, mounted on a carved wooden base. Note the various textures: around the top, the clay was scratched with a comb; the inner part is pierced with many small depressions, made by the end of a pointed tool. The piece is not fired, but is finished by the method described in Chapter 13.

All Figures by Helmut Hirnschall
All photographs by Trevor N. Larden
All pottery illustrated is by Ida Claire Larden,
except where otherwise indicated.
We wish to acknowledge the advice kindly given by Arthur Freeman

Library of Congress Cataloging in Publication Data

Larden, Ida Claire.
    The off-wheel pottery book.

    Bibliography: p.
    1. Pottery craft.   I. Hull, Raymond, 1919-
joint author.   II. Title.
TT920.L37   738.1   74-18321
ISBN 0-684-14110-8

1 3 5 7 9 11 13 15 17 19 C/MD 20 18 16 14 12 10 8 6 4 2

Printed in the United States of America

CONTENTS

Two carved heads and wall plaque. UPPER LEFT: *plaque 3½″ x 6″. The design was worked into the wet clay. Note that the eye-holes go right through; against a white wall, this makes the eyes shine. A hole is made at the top for hanging the piece up. This plaque is glazed green and black, but similar pieces could just as well be biscuit fired and stove-polished.* LOWER LEFT: *figure 10″ high by Arthur Freeman, carved from a solid block of clay. Note how the base and head are hollowed out to avoid excessive thickness of clay, which would present difficulties in drying and firing. Part is glazed, part left unglazed.* LOWER RIGHT: *head 9″ x 4¾″ by Arthur Freeman, mounted on metal rods 4½″ high, set in a wooden base. Holes were made in the head to fit the rods then, after firing, the rods were glued in. This piece is partly glazed, partly unglazed. See Chapter 13.*

No-Wheel Pottery

POTTERY, among the oldest of the arts, can still offer keen personal satisfaction to any one who practices it today. You take a low-cost, abundant raw material—clay—and shape it with your own hands and a few simple tools, into beautiful articles, for practical use, for ornaments, for gifts, or for sale. After working on the projects described in this book, you will be able to create and execute your own designs.

What Is Pottery?

The craft of pottery began thousands of years ago. Someone—perhaps a bright child—noticed the plastic nature of moist clay, and squeezed a piece of it into a new shape. Coming back to this plaything a few days later, after it had dried, he found it could no longer be molded, but was hard and held its shape.

Air-dried clay was adequate for some purposes. As a liner for storage-baskets, it would keep mice out of the food; molded into bricks it would, in a dry climate, make durable walls for houses; clay plastered around eggs would preserve them.

There were two problems. First, if the clay got damp, it would become soft and plastic again; or, if thoroughly wetted, it would turn into a gooey liquid. Second, it was not very strong: under friction it would wear away and, if it got a sharp knock, it would crack and crumble. (The mixing of straw in adobe bricks is a means of countering this brittleness.)

Real pottery-making began when somebody noticed that clay, burned in the fire, was not just drier than the air-dried clay: it had become markedly different. It was much harder; it would withstand a lot of friction without cracking; and, most important, when wetted it did not become soft again. The clay, after firing, had turned into something very much like a piece of stone! (Indeed, pots of fired clay replaced the older pots that were laboriously carved from solid blocks of stone.)

Early potters noticed that some kinds of clay, even after firing, were still porous: water would soak through them. (Bricks and flower-pots are still made like this.) Other kinds of clay, when fired, develop a hard, glossy coating, impervious to liquids (like stone crocks and teapots). Eventually potters learned how to produce a glaze when they wanted it, how to vary its thickness and color, and how to use it for ornament.

These are still the basic stages of the pottery process—the same today as thousands of years ago.

1. Form the moist clay into the shape you want.

2. Let it get *thoroughly* dry. (If you try to fire the pot before it is dry, it will fall to pieces.)

3. Fire it. (We still use the old word "fire," even though nowadays the heat may be applied by an electric or oil-burning kiln.)

No Wheel?

The potter's art, in many people's minds, is inseparably associated with the potter's wheel. Yet excellent pottery was made for many centuries and in many countries, before the potter's wheel was ever invented.

The techniques described in this book will produce work just as strong, just as beautiful, as any turned on a wheel.

These methods save you the cost of a wheel, and the space that a wheel would occupy in your home. They eliminate the mess that a potter's wheel inevitably makes. (With a wheel, the potter himself, and his surroundings always get liberally spattered with a mixture of clay and water.)

For many people, a major objection to the potter's wheel is that its use requires considerable strength in hands, arms and shoulders. In places where the wheel was not used, pottery was freely practiced by women; introduction of the wheel made pottery into a male preserve! The no-wheel techniques that follow require no particular strength unless you are making very large, heavy pots; they can be carried out by young children, even by people who have one hand or arm rather weak (say from arthritis).

With these no-wheel methods, you need no special workroom; you can make pots on an ordinary kitchen table, countertop or pastry-board. When you are finished for the day, your materials and equipment will all go away on one closet shelf.

Ceremonial jar, Northern Sung Dynasty, 960-1226 A. D. Height, 6″
PROPERTY OF MR. & MRS. ARTHUR FREEMAN.

Figure by Arthur Freeman, 17″ tall, carved from a solid block of well-wedged clay. The head was hollowed before finishing. Bronze-colored matt glaze.

2

Equipment

Now let's see what equipment is needed for pottery. Some of the items you already have around the house. The others you can buy cheaply enough at any craft store, or, by following the instructions below, you can make them.

Boards

You need a fairly big flat surface for such operations as wedging and rolling out clay. It's quite practical to use a table, a kitchen counter-top or a pastry-board; but many potters prefer to keep a separate board for their work. If you decide to do that, get a piece of ¾-inch plywood about 2-feet square, with one face clear of knot-holes and sanded smooth; some potters cover the board with a layer of smooth, laminated counter-top material.

For convenient working on individual pots, get a few smaller pieces of board—they may be square or round—about 9 inches to 1 foot across; these small boards are called bats. By making each pot on a bat, you can move it around with no risk of deforming the soft clay: you just pick up the bat with the pot on it, and set it aside to dry.

Cutting Wire

Better than a knife for cutting large lumps of clay is a piece of wire sometimes called a "wedging wire." (The reason for that name appears in Chapter 3.) To make it, get a piece of thin picture-wire (some potters prefer the kind that consists of two strands twisted together) about 18 inches long. Tie the ends to a couple of sticks, each about as thick as your index finger, and about 4 inches long. The wire is knotted around the middle of each stick, making two handles with which you can apply tension to the wire. (Or use two big buttons with the wire tied through them.)

Roller

For rolling out clay into smooth sheets and slabs, there's nothing to beat an ordinary rolling pin. A smooth, round, glass bottle or jar will also serve the purpose.

Cloths

When rolling out clay, you cover the board with a piece of cloth, to prevent the clay from sticking to the wood. A piece of fairly close-woven canvas will give a smooth finish to the clay. Alternatively, if you use a piece of burlap to roll the clay on, you obtain an interesting texture on the clay surface.

In the "hammock" method of forming (described in Chapter 4) a piece of old bed-sheet will give the pot a smooth surface; or a piece of cheesecloth could be used to give a rougher texture.

So an assortment of cloth pieces, from 3-feet square down to about 18-inches square, will come in useful.

Slats

To produce clay slabs of controlled thickness, pairs of wooden slats are used to guide the roller. Each slat is about 18-inches long and 1-wide. You can begin with one pair of slats, ¼-inch in thickness; you'll find it handy to have two more pairs as well, one pair ⅛-inch thick, the other pair ⅜-inch thick.

#1 80-gauge sieve with brush in it; #2 Various brushes for applying glaze and decoration; #3 Stick for stirring glaze; #4 Two cutting wires, one with sticks on ends, one with buttons; #5 Circular wooden bats; #6 Spatula for scraping clay off cutting boards, etc.; #7 Sandpaper; #8 Canvas-covered board.

Towels

For absorbing water from too-wet clay, you need one or two towels. Dish-towels will serve the purpose, or pieces of old terry towel; so will thick paper towels.

Plastic

To keep clay in moist, workable condition until you use it, and to control the drying rate of a finished pot, the handiest thing is a plastic bag. The bags you get vegetables in are perfect. When you go on to bigger projects, you can use plastic garment bags from the cleaners.

Knife

The wedging wire cuts thick lumps of clay, but you'll also need a knife. An ordinary paring knife is good. A knife made specially for cutting and shaping clay is called a fettling tool or fettling knife.

Modeling Tools

Wooden modeling tools are available, about 6 to 8 inches long, with variously shaped blades on the ends. The photo shows a shape that is handy for most purposes.

If you don't want to buy such a tool, you can contrive various substitutes. The handle of a teaspoon (not one that has a raised design on it, of course) will serve; a letter-opener of metal or plastic, a nail-file, the rounded end of a bottle-opener—you can use your ingenuity to improvise.

Another useful modeling tool has two wire loops—one wide, one narrow—on a wooden handle. This can be bought, or made at home from two bobby-pins fastened to a stick with adhesive tape.

A wire cheese-cutter is also handy for modeling.

A fine-tooth comb and a piece of hacksaw blade are useful for roughening the surface of the clay when you want to make a joint between two leather-hard pieces.

An ice-pick, or a carpenter's awl, is good for piercing holes.

Paddle

A strip of wood, 1″ x 2″ and about a foot long, is useful for forming clay, smoothing off uneven surfaces, etc.

Sponges

One small and one large sponge will be useful, for moistening clay, smoothing off surfaces and edges of pots, and for cleaning the surface you have worked your clay on. Natural or cellulose sponges will do; the smaller the holes, the better.

A form of sponge called the "elephant ear" is used by many potters; it is a small, thin, natural sponge with a triangular shape somewhat like that of an elephant's ear.

Ornamental Tools

For impressing or inscribing patterns on a clay surface, you can use such things as the embossed rollers normally used for decorating pastry, butter-patters, combs, saw-blades, knitting needles, and so on.

You can take a piece of wood the same size as your paddle, and make it into an embossing tool by driving some round-headed tacks into one side of it, for two or three inches down from one end; the tacks may be regularly or irregularly spaced, according to the effect you want. You can take a paddle, and nail one or more pop-bottle or beer-bottle tops on it so that it impresses a serrated circle each time you hit the clay. Or you can make patterns on clay with one of those serrated mallets that are used to tenderize meat.

You can take a piece of rough stone or concrete—somewhere from wal-nut-size to egg-size is handy—with one side fairly flat. Pressed into the soft clay all over a pot or tile, it gives an interesting rough texture. Speaking of walnuts suggests that a walnut, pressed with a rolling motion into soft clay, would also produce an attractive texture effect.

Be on the lookout for unconventional uses of ordinary objects. While working on this book, I was shaping a small pot while my collaborator took notes with a ball-point pen. Suddenly I got an idea, borrowed the pen and began pressing the upper end of it vertically into the soft clay! Depending on the pressure, it formed several different depressed patterns. Try it yourself.

Get a block of wood and cover it with burlap, fastened in place with thumb-tacks. By pressing the burlap against soft clay, you can get a text-ured effect.

Here's another tool for creating texture. Get a flat piece of thin metal —the lid of a can will do; lay it on a piece of wood, and punch holes through it with a nail, in regular or irregular pattern. The raised tongues of metal surrounding the holes will form an embossed pattern when you press the piece of metal against soft clay.

Engobe Applicators

Engobe (fully described in Chapter 3) is a decorative material of a thin, creamy texture. You can apply it to unfired pottery, like paint, with a brush; but for making thin lines of engobe, one handy tool is a plastic squeeze-bottle with a fine nozzle. Also good for this purpose is an icing-syringe (of the kind used for icing cakes); such a syringe usually comes equipped with several nozzles of different apertures, so you can use it to make lines of various thickness.

Plaster Bats

These are slabs, 8 or 10 inches across, made from plaster of Paris. They are useful for absorbing water from clay that is too wet for proper working. You can buy them ready-made, quite cheaply, at a ceramic supply store or you can get some plaster of Paris at a hardware store. To mix it, put water into a bowl and sprinkle the plaster on the surface. Let it stand two minutes, then stir it with your hand, fingers apart, in a lifting, scooping motion from the bottom towards the top. The mix is ready for use when it has the consistency of thick cream.

Pie-tins make good molds; grease them before use, and the bats will come out easily. Don't skimp on the plaster; fill the pie-tin right up, so that the bats will be at least one inch thick, for strength and good absorbency. While the plaster is still soft, level off the top of each bat with the edge of a ruler, or some other flat object, to get it perfectly smooth.

Though the newly-cast bats soon get hard, they contain a lot of water; let them dry for several days before use.

Warning! Don't put waste plaster, or a mixture of plaster and water, down the drain; you'll block it up! Clean the bowl in which you mixed the plaster as soon as you have poured into the pie tins; wipe it with old newspapers until every scrap is removed. Rinse your hands, and tools used in the mixing, in a basin of water; then pour that water into an old can or jar and leave it till the plaster has settled to the bottom and solidified. Then you can pour off the water and throw the can into the garbage.

#1 Rolling pin; #2 Carving tools; #3 Sponges, one elephant ear, one synthetic; #4 Plastic turntable; #5 Fettling tool; #6 Plastic ruler; #7 Dividers; #8 Canvas-covered board; #9 Wooden slats for rolling clay slabs.

Sieve or Screen

For making your own glazes and engobes, and for some other operations in potting, it's useful to have a fine sieve. The size I recommend is 80 gauge: that means that it has 80 holes to the inch. You can buy a sieve ready to use; or, if you are handy with tools, you can save a little money by getting a square foot of the 80-gauge screen, and mounting it in a home-made wooden frame.

Scales

You do not need scales to start with. I would advise that you begin by using glazes and engobes obtained ready-mixed from the store. But when you are ready to start making your own glazes and engobes, you will need accurate scales. Recipes are usually given in grams; for best results, they must be followed accurately; so your scales should weigh down to 1/10 gram (i.e. about 1/300 oz.). Ordinary kitchen scales, or even postal scales, just aren't accurate enough!

The scale should be strong enough to weigh up to somewhat over 300 grams (i.e. about 12 ozs.). Many potters feel that 300 grams is a good batch; it's worth the trouble of making it up, not just for one job, but to keep some in store for future use. A good ceramic supply store will have such scales in stock, or can get them for you. They are not cheap; but, for the advanced potter, can be a good investment.

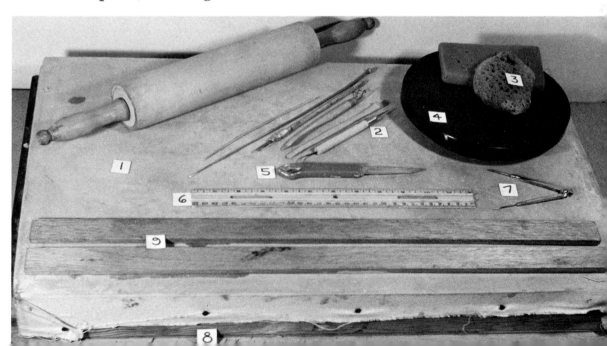

3

Clay

CLAY consists of microscopically fine crystals of rock that has been decomposed by natural forces such as pressure, heat, water and frost.

The most important ingredients of clay are silicon, aluminum, oxygen and water. The different kinds of clay have these elements in different proportions; they also have small, differing proportions of other elements such as iron, magnesium, calcium, sodium and potassium.

There's no need to discuss in detail the effects of all these ingredients; but we should mention two of them, iron and water.

Clay and Iron
The iron content of clay largely determines the color of the finished pot after firing. Less than 1 percent iron (in the form of iron oxide) usually gives a white color; 1 percent to 2 percent or thereabouts gives a cream color; 4 percent gives a light red; 7 percent a rich, brick-red color.

Clay and Water
In clay, water can be present in two forms. First, take a piece of unfired clay that is apparently perfectly dry; it may have been standing for weeks in a warm room. Yet it still contains water (usually about 10 percent to 15 percent depending on what kind of clay it is); but this water is chemically

combined with the other elements of the clay, and cannot be removed by ordinary drying methods. We call this the "combined water."

This combined water can be removed only by firing; when the clay is red-hot (about 700°C., 1292°F.) it will all be gone. Once the clay has been fired, and the combined water thus removed, no amount of soaking will put it back; the fired clay will never become soft again.

Now let's consider the other form of water. Take that dry piece of unfired clay and add water to it, giving it plenty of time to soak in. The clay absorbs more and more water, gradually becoming soft and plastic. If you stop adding water and give the clay time to dry out, it gradually stiffens and becomes hard again.

This part of the water content that controls the hardness or softness of the clay is called the "water of plasticity," or "mechanical water." The mechanical water can be added and removed as often as you like, to make the clay softer or harder. (That's in contrast with the combined water which, once removed, cannot be replaced.)

PROPERTIES OF CLAY

There are several things a potter wants to know about a sample of clay.

1. How well can I work it? That is, how easily will it yield to my fingers and tools to take the shape I want? Will it hold that shape after I have finished working it?

2. How much will it shrink in drying (i.e. in losing the mechanical water)? Some clays shrink 10 percent or more; so a vase originally shaped to stand 10 inches high would be only 9 inches high when dry. For some kinds of work—making ornamental tiles, for example—it may be important to know, and to allow for this shrinkage.

3. What temperature is required to fire it properly? How much additional shrinkage will there be in firing (i.e. in losing the combined water and other chemical changes)? What will be its color and texture after it is fired?

TYPES OF CLAY

There are many different kinds of clay; here are a few of the most important ones.

Kaolin or China clay produces a white pot when fired; but it is not easy to work with, and it requires a very high firing temperature. Used by itself, it cannot be recommended for the kind of work described in this book; but it can be an important ingredient when mixed with other substances.

Ball clay—so called because it used to be sold in balls—is usually gray in color, because it contains minute particles of decayed vegetable matter. It is very plastic, and strong when dry; yet it shrinks so much in drying and firing that it is seldom used by itself, but is generally blended with other clays or non-clay materials.

Stoneware clay contains considerable quantities of a mineral called feldspar. It works easily, and produces strong, hard, watertight pots, in a range of colors from gray to red-brown. (The "stone crock" is actually of stoneware.) But this clay requires a high firing temperature, and should be used only by experienced potters.

Brick clay produces red, porous pots when fired (flower pots, for example).

"Pottery clay," as sold in craft stores, is for use with a wheel; it is very fine-grained and smooth. It is not suitable for no-wheel techniques, except on small items—say a dish or ashtray not more than 5 inches across; it could also be used for the "hammock" technique. (Chapter 4.)

"Modeling clay," sometimes called "Sculpture clay" or "terra cotta clay" is the kind we want to use. It is a mixture of clay with a proportion of grog. Grog is clay that has been fired, and then crushed to powder. Because of the grog content, this clay is less sticky than pottery clay, and therefore easier to work with; it holds its shape well, and is less likely than softer clays to sag during drying; it shrinks less in drying and in firing than some of the pure clays.

BUYING CLAY

Clay is usually sold, moist, in a condition just about ready to use, in cardboard cartons or plastic bags. Twenty-five pounds is the smallest economical quantity. (Some stores will sell less, but at a higher price per pound.)

Clay improves with aging (like wine); so it's worth while to get some extra, and always hold a supply in reserve. Best results will be obtained from the aging process if you leave the clay (still tightly closed in its bag or carton) exposed to outdoor temperature changes—in a garden shed, or on a balcony, for example.

(So important is this aging that the old-time Chinese potter would use clay that had been prepared by his father, and in turn he would prepare clay to be used by his own son.)

WEDGING

Wedging is a process that serves two important purposes. It distributes moisture equally through a lump of clay. (You can't work the clay properly if some parts of it are wetter than others.) Wedging also removes any air bubbles that might be in the clay. (If you left those bubbles in, they would create weak spots in your finished pot.)

Here's how to do it:

1. Take a piece of clay about the size of your two fists. *Immediately* put the remainder of your clay back into the plastic bag it came in, and fasten the neck. (This is an important rule: keep spare clay in a closed plastic bag; never leave it lying around exposed to the drying action of the air.)

2. By banging it on the board, shape your piece of clay into a rough rectangular shape. Slam it down firmly enough so that it sticks to the board; then, with a horizontal movement of your cutting wire, slice it in halves.

3. Pick up the bottom half and slap it down again, fairly hard, with the cut side up, so that it flattens out somewhat.

4. Slap the other half hard down on top of it, with the cut side up. The two pieces are now blended into one lump again.

5. Stand the lump on end and cut it in half again.

6. Slap the two halves down again, cut sides up, as before.

7. Repeat the cutting and slapping process about 10 times. This is usually enough. On the last few cuts, check the cut faces for any remaining air bubbles.

With a little practice, you'll find that you can do this wedging quite quickly. It *must* be done *every time* you begin to work, either with a new batch of clay, or with old clay that has been held in storage.

Some people prefer to cut downward with the wire instead of horizontally. This makes no difference to the end result.

One point for apartment-dwellers. The slapping down of the lumps of clay makes a loud banging on the board. If you particularly want to avoid noise, you can press the lumps firmly together with your hand, instead of throwing them down. Knead the clay mass a few times (like kneading dough) then cut it again and repeat the process. This method takes a little longer, but the operation is silent.

MOISTURE CONTROL

It's essential that the clay, when you start to use it, should contain just the right amount of moisture. If it's too wet, it will stick to your fingers and tools; even if you persist in working it, the finished piece won't hold its shape. If the clay is too dry, you can't shape it properly; instead of yielding smoothly to pressure, it will crack and crumble.

So every time you start work, wedge your clay first, then test it for moisture and, if necessary, remove the excess or make up the deficiency.

The Moisture Test

Take a piece of clay the size of a small egg, and roll it between your hands. If it has the right moisture content, it will form a smooth cigar shape. If it is too wet, it sticks to your hands. If it is too dry, it will crumble.

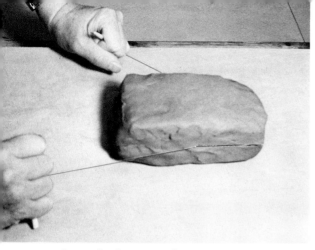

Making the horizontal cut.

Slapping down the top half.

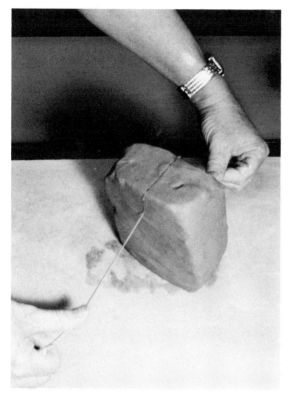

Cutting downward.

Kneading clay.

If it is too wet or too dry, press the test piece back into the main lump and follow whichever of the following procedures is needed.

Clay Too Wet

Lay the lump of clay on the board; roll it back and forth a few times to form a thick cylinder; then, with the cutting wire, cut it into slices about 1-inch thick. Lay these slices on a towel (terry, linen or paper) and gently press another towel on top of them. The towels will absorb excess water from the clay. Alternatively, cut the clay in two or three pieces and lay them, flat side down, on plaster bats, which will quickly absorb excess water. After a few minutes repeat the moisture test. If the moisture content is now correct, you can begin to work.

If the clay is still too wet, press all the slices firmly together into one lump; cut it again into slices (this time at right angles to the direction of the first cuts) and again lay the slices between towels, or on plaster bats.

After three or four minutes, test again.

Clay Too Dry

With the cutting wire, cut the clay into slices 1-inch thick. Poke your finger 5 or 6 times into each slice, to make holes about ¾-inch deep. Sprinkle water over the slices—just enough to wet them—letting a little water into the holes (not enough to fill them up, though!).

Now press the slices together into one lump; wedge the clay till the water is uniformly distributed, then make the moisture test again.

SALVAGING DRIED-OUT CLAY

The method described above under "Clay Too Dry" applies to clay that is too dry for satisfactory working, but that still has enough moisture in it to be in some degree plastic.

You may sometimes have to deal with clay that has completely dried out. Perhaps you have formed a pot and, after it is dry, yet before it is fired, you decide you don't like it. Or, through too-rapid drying, a pot may warp or crack; or a fully-dried, unfired pot may get accidentally broken.

Then here's how to salvage the clay. Break the hard, dry clay into pieces about 1 inch across (use the rolling pin or a piece of wood to crack it). Put them in a bowl and add water—just enough barely to cover the clay. Leave it 24 hours to absorb the water. It will now be quite soft. Press it into a lump, wedge it, test for moisture content, and make whatever correction is necessary, as described above.

MAKING SLIP

Slip is a mixture of clay and water, about the consistency of glue, that is used for sticking clay surfaces together—for example, sticking a handle on a cup.

When you are going to make a batch of slip, leave some pieces of clay —for example, the waste pieces cut off a pot you are forming—out to get thoroughly dry, instead of putting them back in the plastic bag as usual.

When the time comes to make the slip, break the clay into small pieces, about the size of your little fingernail. In a wide-mouth jar or small mixing bowl put about ½ inch of water, then gradually sprinkle in the broken clay. You'll notice that it slowly absorbs the water. *Don't stir* the mixture till all the water has been absorbed. (This may take 2 hours for a small batch, longer for a big one.) Then stir thoroughly and, if necessary, add more water, a little at a time, till the mixture is of the proper glue-like consistency.

You can store a batch of slip indefinitely in a jar with a tight-fitting screw lid. Always stir before use.

To apply slip to a small area, use a water-color brush, or the corner of a sponge.

SPECIAL MIXTURES

For certain kinds of work, special ingredients may have important advantages. Here are several such formulas.

Egyptian Paste

The two forms of Egyptian paste described below are particularly useful for making ceramic jewelry. The ingredients can be bought at any ceramic supply store. They are quite cheap. You don't need large quantities, so get the smallest amount the store will sell, usually ¼ lb or ½ lb.

Matt Finish

The basic formula:

> Silica, 4 tablespoons (level)
> Bentonite, 4 teaspoons (Bentonite is a kind of clay)
> Bicarbonate of soda, 2 teaspoons
> Copper carbonate, ½ teaspoon
> Lead frit, 1 tablespoon

Mix the ingredients thoroughly with water, till the consistency is right for proper working. Spare quantities of the mixture can be kept in a screw-top jar.

This basic mixture would give a neutral, grayish color when fired. For more attractive colors, add ingredients as follows:

For gray-green, add to the basic formula ½ teaspoon copper oxide.

For robin's-egg blue, add to the basic formula ¼ teaspoon cobalt oxide.

You can experiment with adding other coloring ingredients; but many potters find it difficult to get good results with them.

Articles made with this mixture will not stick to each other in firing.

Glossy Finish

This mixture forms a glaze in one firing.

> Feldspar, 3 tablespoons
> China clay, 2 tablespoons
> Flint, 1½ tablespoons
> Fine white sand, 2½ teaspoons
> Bicarbonate of soda, 2 teaspoons
> Soda ash, 2 teaspoons
> Ball clay, 1½ teaspoons
> Whiting, 1½ teaspoons

This is the basic mixture. To obtain attractive colors, add the same ingredients as for the matt paste.

Pieces made of this mixture will stick to anything they touch in firing —to each other, or to the kiln shelf; so take the precautions described in Chapter 7.

Egyptian paste can be bought ready-made at many good ceramic supply stores, and save the trouble of measuring and mixing the ingredients.

Engobe

Engobe is a decorative material which is painted onto a pot at the leather-hard stage. Then, after drying is finished and the pot is fired, the pot will be colored. Because clay forms a major part of the mixture, I describe it in this chapter. ("Engobe" is a French word. It can be pronounced as it is spelled; but some potters prefer the French pronunciation *Ahng-gobe.*)

Engobes in dry powder form, to be mixed with water, or ready-mixed for use, are available in many colors from ceramic supply stores. I would recommend that you begin with the ready-to-use forms.

Later, you may want to go on to mixing your own engobes. Here are some formulas. First, the basic recipe that, after firing, produces a white layer.

China clay (Kaolin)	25 grams
Ball clay	20 grams
Flint	30 grams
Feldspar	17 grams
Whiting	2 grams
Magnesium carbonate	6 grams

All the ingredients are dry powders. Put them in a mixing bowl and gradually add cold water, stirring all the time (I find a 1″ paint brush convenient for stirring), till the mixture has a thin, creamy consistency. Then pass it through the 80-mesh sieve, working any lumps through the mesh with the brush, till the whole batch is uniformly smooth.

Store in a screw-top jar. Stir well each time before use.

To produce colors, add the following ingredients to this basic mixture:

For blue, add ¾ gram cobalt oxide.

For greeny-blue, add 3 grams copper oxide.

For red-brown, add 8 grams red iron oxide.

For yellow, add 3 grams yellow under-glaze color.

For turquoise, add 3 grams copper carbonate and ½ gram cobalt oxide.

For black, add 2 grams red iron oxide, 2 grams manganese dioxide and 2½ grams cobalt oxide.

These are the colors I use most; but ceramic supply stores have many other underglaze colors that you can experiment with.

(Note that the additives do not color the engobe at the time of mixing: the color develops only after firing.)

You can get a considerable variation in color intensity by applying different numbers of coats. One coat of engobe, when dried and fired, will usually let the color of the body of the pot show through to some extent. For a more intense color, paint on one coat of engobe; let it dry (that should take only a few minutes), then apply a second coat. For a still greater intensity, let the second coat dry and apply a third.

Of course, you don't have to use the same number of coats all over a pot; variations of color intensity can provide an interesting element of design. A few experiments will show you the kind of effects that can be achieved.

This method of coloring is different from glazing; it produces, in one firing, a thin layer of colored clay on the surface of the pot. This layer is matt in texture, like other fired, unglazed clays. If you want to leave the pot unglazed, fire to cone 04 (cone numbers are explained in Chapter 6); this will bring out the color values. You can somewhat heighten the colors by applying clear varnish, a clear wax polish, or clear nail polish.

But for the best color effect, fire first to cone 06, apply transparent glaze, and fire again to cone 04.

NOTE: some potters talk about this process as "slip coloring," "slip decoration" or a similar term; that's because the engobe mixture contains clay and water, and looks much like slip. But to avoid confusion I shall use the name "slip" exclusively for the clay-water mixture that is used as an adhesive; the decorative mixture described in this section will be referred to as engobe.

Three strip-formed pots. On the tallest pot, at left, a design was painted with copper oxide; then glaze was applied thick and thin to produce the variegated finish. See Chapter 8.

4

Slab Forming

Now let's begin making some pots. In this technique you first make a thin slab of clay. Cut from this slab the outline of the piece you want, then shape it to its final form. This chapter describes several different ways of treating the cutout slab.

FREE-FORM DISHES

For this project you need a slab of clay ¼″ thick all over. Cover the board with a piece of canvas or cloth stretched smooth; this prevents the clay from sticking to the board. Take a ball of freshly-wedged clay about 4 inches in diameter and slap it down in the middle of the board so that it forms a flattish lump. Shape it roughly into a rectangle with your hand, then take the rolling pin and begin to roll it out.

Don't expect to get the clay down to ¼″ thickness in one operation. Roll from the center of the lump towards the ends and sides. If some clay sticks to the roller, wipe it clean with a wet sponge, dry it, and then apply a dusting of talcum powder to the roller; that should prevent further sticking.

After a little while you find that the clay won't spread any further, because it has stuck to the canvas. So lift up one corner of the clay, then another, to loosen it; lift the whole piece of clay clear of the canvas, turn it over and put it down again; then you can roll some more.

This rolling from both sides helps to produce the compact, uniform texture that you need. Each time you turn the slab over, watch for air bubbles in the clay; if you see one, prick it with a pin, and with your fingers smooth some clay in from around it to fill the hole.

Repeat the rolling and turning process till the slab is a little more than ¼″ thick. Now lay two ¼″ wooden slats on the canvas, parallel, one on each side of the slab, and continue rolling till both ends of the roller ride smoothly on the slats all the way across the slab. Now you have a uniform slab of clay, exactly ¼″ thick, and about 1 foot across.

Put a piece of newspaper or a paper towel over the slab, and lay a bat (smaller piece of board) on top of the paper. Pick up the "sandwich" and turn it over; lift off the big board, peel off the canvas, and now the slab is on the bat, ready for cutting.

Cutting The Shape

Rule one-inch squares on a piece of cardboard; then draw on it one of the shapes from the diagram and cut around it to make a template. (It's really best to do this in advance, so that the clay won't dry out while you are making the template.) Lay the template on your clay slab and cut around it with the point of a knife. Now you have the basic shape for your pot.

Rolling slab between slats on canvas-covered board.

Lift the waste clay from outside the cut, put it into a plastic bag, and roll over or tie up the mouth of the bag. If you leave spare clay lying around to get dried out, you make extra work for yourself later in getting it back to proper condition of moisture.

Shaping The Sides

Lift up the edges of the slab to form the sides of a shallow dish. With thumbs inside and fingers outside, turn up the outer inch of clay into a smooth curve, so that the edge is vertical, or nearly so.

Work your way, section by section, right around the slab. When you have the sides shaped to your satisfaction, take a damp sponge and gently wipe with it to remove finger-marks inside and out; finally use the sponge to smooth off the edge. Glaze will not hold on a sharp edge such as that produced by cutting the clay slab with a knife. That's why it's always good practice to pass a sponge over all sharp edges and corners and slightly round them off. (Look at commercially-made cups, pots and dishes; you'll find all edges and corners treated in this way.)

Now you have a pot that, after drying and firing, will make a candy-dish or ashtray. Don't attempt to remove the pot from where it stands on the paper-covered bat, but leave it there to dry. (You can, of course, lift the bat and carry it, pot and all, to the place where drying will be done.) For detailed hints on drying, see Chapter 5.

By the way, with this process, or any other, if you want to make two or more articles exactly alike—perhaps you want one for yourself and one for a gift—it's wise to make them at the same time, from the same batch of clay, then dry and fire them together. Only in this way can you be sure that they will turn out the same.

Suitable shapes for free-form dishes.

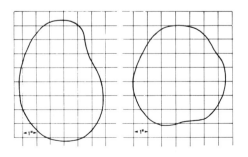

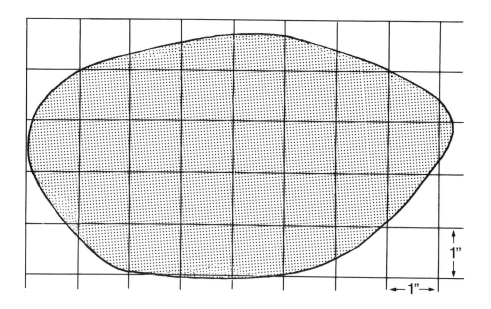

1"

1"

Outline and completed shape of free-form dish.

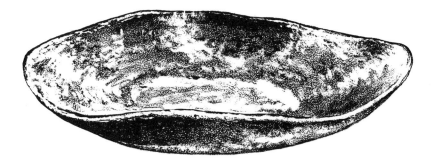

Free-form dishes. LEFT AND CENTER; *sgraffito designs, filled in with black, transparent glaze.* RIGHT; *one glaze applied smoothly, another spattered on with a brush.*

THE FLARE

The next project is to make a rectangular dish with flared sides. So prepare a cardboard template of the size and shape you want. 7″ x 7″ or 6″ x 8½″ are good sizes.

Put a ball of freshly-wedged clay about 5 inches in diameter on the canvas-covered board. Roll out a slab as before, but this time use slats about ⅜″ thick, to give a slightly thicker, stronger slab. Transfer the slab to a bat, with paper underneath, then apply the template and cut out the shape.

Now, with some of the spare clay, roll out four cylindrical pieces, about as thick as your first finger, and about 2″ shorter than the sides of your dish.

Bend up one side of the dish, put one of the cylinders against it, then flare out the side so that it rests on the cylinder.

Proceed in the same way with the other three sides.

Forming flared dish with supporting cylinders in place.

Don't press or work the main piece together with these supporting cylinders; as the clay dries, they will separate. Smooth off fingermarks and edges with a sponge, as before.

One dish that I made by this process has had a number of uses, as candy-dish, ashtray, and also as a baking-dish for meat loaf!

Flared dishes. All had one glaze applied uniformly; then designs painted on in a lighter or darker glaze before the glaze firing.

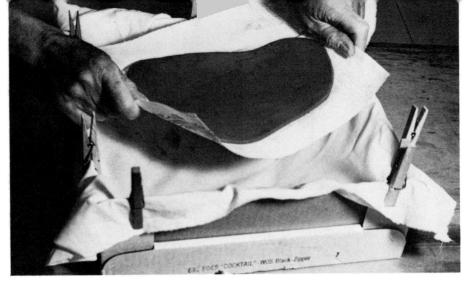

The cut-out form, on a towel, is lowered into the hammock.

The clay form in the hammock; note how the finger and thumb at the left are raising one edge of the clay to shape the side of the dish. The cardboard template used in cutting out the clay form lies to the right of the hammock.

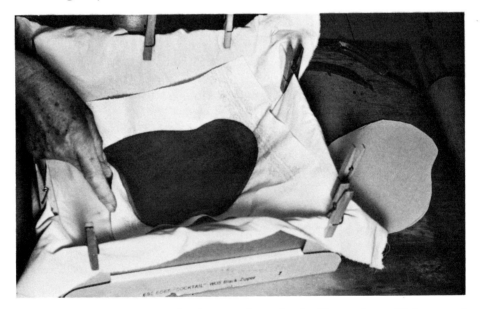

Three pots made by the hammock method; all are about 8″ long and ¼″ thick. UPPER: *The design was painted on the dried greenware with copper oxide and water. Before the second firing a transparent, pale green glaze was applied.* LOWER LEFT: *dark green glaze was applied before the second firing.* LOWER RIGHT: *this is a piece of greenware, showing the variety of form attainable by this method.*

THE HAMMOCK

Get a cardboard carton about 15" square and about 4" deep. Take a piece of cloth about 2-feet square (it can be smooth if you like; or cheesecloth will make an interesting texture on the outside of the finished pot) and fasten it with clothespins to the edge of the carton so that it hangs down inside like a hammock, touching the bottom in the middle. If, as in many cartons, there is a joint or ridge in the middle of the bottom, cover it with a flat piece of wood or card, so that your pot will have a flat base and will stand properly when finished.

Roll out a slab of clay ¼" thick. Cut from it one of the shapes shown on p. 26 or some other shape of your own design, about 6 to 8 inches across.

Now put the cut-out piece of clay into the center of the hammock. Be sure it touches bottom over an area of several square inches.

For a more interesting-looking pot, don't rely solely on the natural sag of the cloth: push it around a little, to give the clay a non-symmetrical shape—curved more sharply at one end than the other, for example, or with the sides more sharply curved than the ends.

To dry a pot in the hammock, wrap a sheet of plastic right around the box. Leave the pot in the hammock till it is leather-hard; then you can take it out to finish drying, and release the hammock for further use. (For full details on drying, see Chapter 5).

CHECKER BOARD AND MEN

The dimensions suggested here will produce a convenient-sized checker set; of course you can, if you like, make the board and men proportionately bigger or smaller.

The Board

Roll out four slabs of clay, each ¼" thick and about 7" square. Each of these is going to make one quarter of your board. (A board made all in one piece would be too big for many kilns.)

Make a cardboard template 6" square; cutting around it with a knife, make four slabs, each exactly 6" square. With the point of a small steel knitting needle, scribe very shallow lines to divide each 6" square into sixteen 1½" squares.

Now set the slabs aside, as described in Chapter 5, to dry till they are leather-hard. During this drying process, turn the slabs over twice a day, to prevent them from drying faster on one side than the other; that would make them warp. To turn a slab without bending it, put a piece of newspaper on the slab, and a bat on top of that; turn over the "sandwich" of two bats and the clay slab; take off the bat and newspaper that were formerly underneath and are now on top.

The Men

Make a circular cardboard template 1¼" in diameter. Roll out a clay slab ⅜" thick and with the template and a sharp knife cut out 24 disks. Set them aside similarly to dry till leather-hard.

The Colors

Make up a batch of black engobe. When board and men are leather-hard, paint alternate squares of the board with it, using a small paint brush. The first coat will be absorbed in a few minutes; then apply a second coat. Wait till it, too, is absorbed, then apply a third coat. This will give you a good, deep, black color after firing. If at any time you accidentally get some of the engobe on to a square that should be left natural-colored, just wipe it off with the corner of a sponge, or a piece of cloth. If that doesn't remove it all, scrape away the remainder with the point of a knife and, with a spoon or modeling tool, smooth off any roughness. Now set the squares aside, as described in Chapter 5, for final drying.

Examine the men. If there are any rough spots around the edges, smooth them out with a modeling tool.

Give three coats of black engobe to the tops and edges of half the men. Set these aside for one day, then turn them over and similarly give three coats to the other face. Set aside for final drying.

WIND CHIMES

To make wind chimes, roll out a slab ¼" thick, and cut out a number of shapes. You can use some of the shapes shown here, or design your own.

Let them dry till leather-hard, then bore a hole in each one with a knitting needle, nail or ice-pick. At this time you can also, if you wish, carve incised designs on the chimes.

You can finish the drying, fire them, and leave them in their natural color; you can color them with engobe when leather-hard; or you can fire them twice, with a plain or colored glaze applied before the second firing.

Suitable shapes for wind chimes.

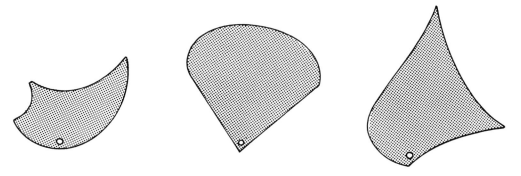

Wind chimes by Gisela Kaempffer. The big circles are about 2½″ across. The clay is about ¼″ thick, and the rings are about ⅜″ wide from inner to outer edge. These are not pierced with holes; the plastic thongs are simply knotted on to the rings. Note that they are mounted so that they will knock against each other when the wind moves them.

TILES

Tiles are among the easiest things to make, yet they offer great scope for creativity. They can be used for fireplaces, table-tops or wall-plaques; a single tile can serve as a tea-pot stand or coaster.

Let's look at the general procedure. Roll out a slab of clay ⅜″ thick, and cut out pieces of the size and shape you want. If you are making tiles to fit a certain area, remember that they are going to shrink somewhat in the drying and firing. (Of course, you can fill in the gaps with grout, but you don't want those gaps to look too big.) So cut the tiles about 5 percent bigger than the finished dimensions you want.

There are many ways of making relief patterns. In the soft clay you can make embossed designs with your fingers, the end of a pencil, the end of a candle, coins, a bottle-cap, a bottle-neck, a ruler, a vegetable grater, and so on.

Carefully turn the tile over and with the incising tool cut several shallow, parallel grooves in the back of it.

Then put the tiles under plastic to dry. An important point for drying tiles is that, even under plastic, they will tend to dry faster on the upper than on the lower side. If you don't check that tendency, the tiles will warp in drying, and stay warped after they are dry. The remedy is to turn them over twice daily till they are leather-hard. To turn tiles without bending them, use the two-bats "sandwich" method described earlier in this chapter for the checker board.

Group of three tiles for wall plaque, with grooves incised on reverse side.

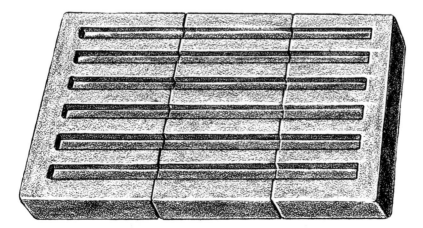

Another problem: the edges of a tile may dry faster than the middle; if you see this happening, run a damp sponge around the edges once a day.

At the leather-hard stage, you can make incised patterns with a knife or wire-loop tool.

Also, at this stage you can apply engobe, in several different ways:

(a) Uniformly over the whole tile;

(b) In different intensities of the same color (obtained by different numbers of coats);

(c) In two or more different colors.

Then you finish the drying, fire the tiles and, if you wish, apply a glaze and fire again.

Cutting incised pattern on a leather-hard tile with the wire-loop tool. For cutting long straight lines, it would be desirable to guide the tool with a ruler. The beginner might find it useful to draw the pattern on paper before beginning to cut the clay.

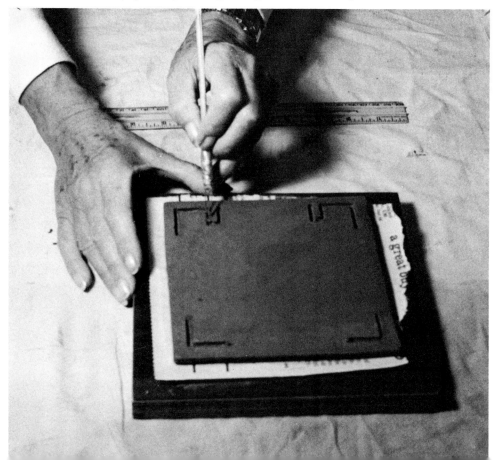

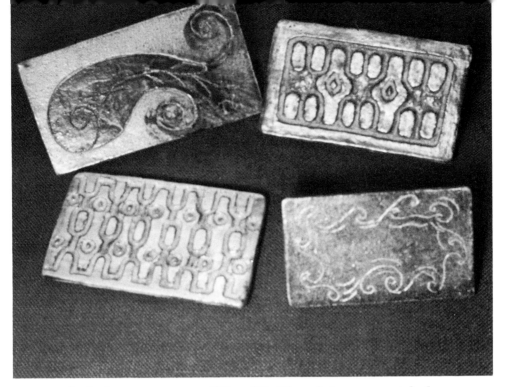

Four finished tiles. UPPER LEFT: *7½″ x 4¼″. The whale was scratched with a fine knitting needle and the form filled in with engobe.* UPPER RIGHT: *6⅜″ x 4″. This is an example of the applied design" technique in which the segments are stuck to the body of the tile with slip.* LOWER RIGHT: *5⅝″ x 3½″. The tile was first covered with a dark engobe, then the sgraffito design was scratched in it.* LOWER LEFT: *6⅜″ x 4″. Incised carving with bobby-pin tool.*

APPLIED CLAY DESIGN

This technique can be used for creating a raised design on any clay surface—a tile, a bowl, a vase, etc. I would suggest, though, that you begin by trying the method a few times on tiles, to get used to it.

First roll out a slab ⅜″ thick, and cut out a tile 8″ x 5″. Now roll out another slab ⅛″ thick, and with a ready-prepared paper template, cut out a group of design elements. With slip, stick them in place on the body of the tile.

If you want a color contrast, you can apply engobe either to the tile, or to the raised design elements.

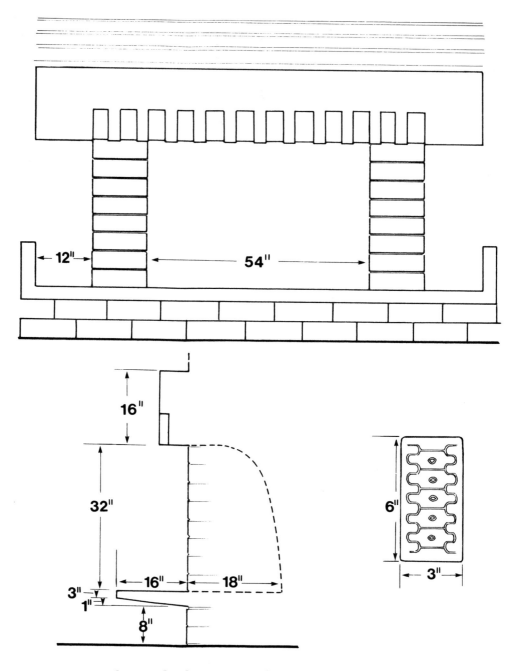

Fireplace with tile insets, in the home of Mr. & Mrs. W. Neil Holman; Roger Kemble, architect; tiles by Ida C. Larden.

Detail of tile fireplace. Incised pattern; satin matt glaze.

Mounting Tiles

Here's an easy way to mount tiles on a table top, plaque or other flat surface.

Get some waterproof linoleum cement; you can buy it at any hardware store in cans from half-pint size up. Note that there are different varieties of this cement, with different requirements for use; so *read the instructions* on the label before you even open the can!

Also get a linoleum cement spreader. There are two forms: one is a rectangular metal sheet with one edge serrated, and a rounded grip on the opposite edge; but a more convenient form has a triangular metal blade, about 3″ wide, mounted in a wooden handle like a paint-brush handle.

Linoleum cement spreader.

The surface that is to support the tiles must be smooth, clean and dry. If necessary, sandpaper down any rough spots. Pour a little cement on the surface and push it around with the spreader. Keep the teeth of the tool hard against the surface; you want to leave a series of narrow ridges of cement, formed by the notches. Cover the whole surface evenly in this way.

Give the cement time to get tacky. (The label on the can tells you how long is needed for the type of cement you are using.) Then set the tiles. It's best to get each one exactly in place, then press it down firmly. Don't try to adjust the position of the tiles by sliding them back and forth on the cement. Allow two days for thorough drying of the cement.

That's the basic method if the tiles are to be closely set. If you want to space the tiles apart and put grout between them, proceed as follows:

Apply the cement as described above; but when putting the tiles in place, space them ⅛″ apart each way. You can use pieces of ⅛″ wooden slats, temporarily placed between adjacent tiles, to achieve uniform spacing. (Take the slats out as soon as each tile is pressed down.) Let the cement dry thoroughly.

Get some tile grouting powder; it's available in small packages in hardware stores. Mix a small amount according to directions on the packages, and fill the spaces between the tiles. Smooth the grout with your hand, with a rubber squeegee—anything that will level it off—flush with the tile surface. The grout gets smeared all over the tiles, but don't worry about that for now. Let it set for a few minutes, then wipe it off the tiles with a damp cloth or sponge.

MOBILES

This is an easy project, good for young children. Make cardboard templates of the animals shown here.

You can design your own animals, birds, fishes or abstract shapes if you like. One thing to watch for is the placement of the hole; make it so that the animal will hang level.

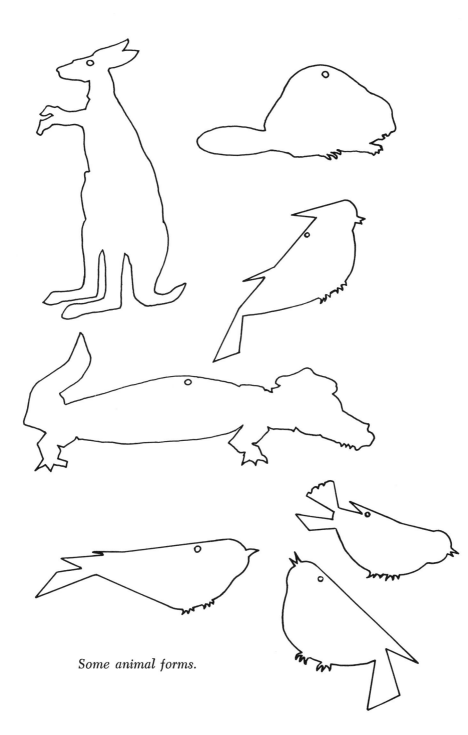

Some animal forms.

Roll out a slab of clay ⅛″ thick, apply the templates and cut out the animals with a knife. (Alternatively, children can cut out shapes with cookie-cutters.) I would not recommend doing much detail-work to suggest fur, feathers, scales, etc.; it's enough to pierce holes for eyes where necessary.

Cover the pieces with plastic and dry till leather-hard. Then, with a knitting-needle or awl, pierce the holes for suspension. At this stage, test, by putting a needle through the hole, to see whether the figure balances properly. If not, correct the balance by shaving a little clay from the heavy end.

Cover loosely with plastic again till drying is complete. Now's the time to consider application of color: you can do designs with underglaze colors (see Chapter 10) on both sides; the two sides can be the same, or different (*e.g.* one side smiling, the other scowling.) Then give a biscuit firing to cone 06. Glazing is optional; even if you don't glaze, the colored designs will still show up well.

For young children, it's best not to let them use the underglaze colors. Biscuit-fire the pieces first, then let the children color them with wax crayons, watercolors, latex paints or poster paints. Then, for a simple glaze substitute, apply clear floor-polish. (Two coats of polish give a higher gloss.)

For hanging the figures, get some nylon thread, or thin wire of suitable thickness at a craft store; or you can get some 14-gauge single-strand copper wire at an electrical store, and strip the insulation off.

Cut it into pieces of different lengths, from 6″ to 9″. With a pair of fine-nosed pliers, twist a small loop at both ends of each piece.

There's just one trick to making a mobile hang properly: start at the bottom and work up. Suppose you have four figures. Hang nos. 1 and 2 from both ends of the first wire. Find the balancing point, near the middle of the wire and there tie a thread 6″ long. Fix it in place with a drop of glue.

Tie the end of this thread to one end of the second wire. From the other end of the wire hang animal no. 3. Find the balancing point and there tie and glue another 6″ thread.

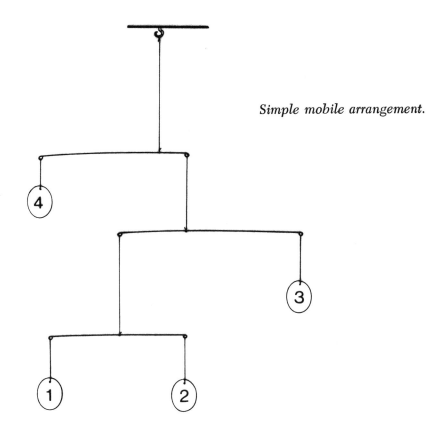

Simple mobile arrangement.

Tie this thread to one end of the third wire. On the other end of this wire, hang animal no. 4. Find the balancing point, and there tie and glue the thread by which you hang the whole thing.

This is the simplest way of setting up a mobile. If you have more figures, the structure can be more elaborate. For example, at one end of a wire, instead of having just one figure, you can hang a wire that supports two figures. Or you could make the four-figure group described above and balance that with a five-figure group at opposite ends of a thicker piece of wire. There's great scope for ingenuity here.

For pre-schoolers, you could make a mobile using numbered disks or shapes instead of animals—something like the diagram above.

(Note: if you are using copper wire for cross-pieces, and you find it bends too much, lay it on a board, and tap all along it with a hammer; that stiffens and tempers it.)

NAME-PLATES OR NUMBER-PLATES

Number-plates or name-plates for your front door are easily made from clay slabs. First draw the name or number, full-size. Roll out a slab ⅜″ thick and cut it to the size you require. When it is leather-hard, trace the inscription on it; with the wire loop cutter, cut away the surrounding clay about ⅛″, leaving the letters or numerals standing up. Bore the screw holes (and countersink them if necessary).

Finish drying and biscuit-fire to cone 06. Apply a light glaze to the background and a black one to the inscription (or vice versa) and fire again to cone 04.

PORTER

Here's the figure of a little man carrying a big basket. By the hole in his hat, he hangs on a nail, and the basket makes a handy storage place for little odds and ends.

The porter is a good project for a child, to be cut in two parts from a ¼″ slab. Form the basket to shape, and weld it with thumb and fingers to the main body part, while the clay is soft.

When the clay is leather-hard, cut the eyes and mouth, shape the hands, and with a coarse-tooth comb, indicate texture on the basket.

The porter, finished.

I would not recommend trying to make a realistic face, but a child can of course carve a face different from that shown in the diagram.

When the piece is fully dried, it can be painted with two or more colors of engobe or underglaze colors before firing. Alternatively, it can be fired as it is, and then the child can color it with wax crayons.

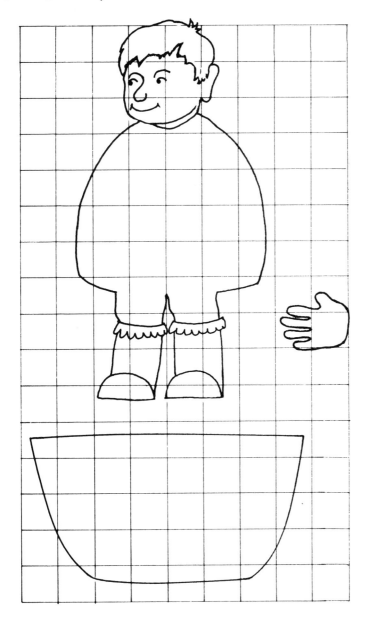

The porter, outline.

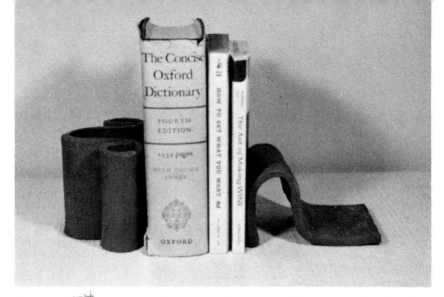

Book ends. Note the effective results obtainable simply by bending slabs of clay.

Design for plaque of three tiles. Note that in this project holes are bored in each tile to take screws for firm mounting on the wall, or on a board.

5

Drying

You have finished shaping a pot from moist, plastic clay; now let's discuss the next process.

Why Dry?
A piece of clay must be dried before it is fired; any attempt to fire it before it is fully dry will simply make it explode, as the mechanical water in the clay turns to steam. The purpose of drying, then, is to remove as much as possible of that mechanical water before firing begins.

Warping and Cracking
As I mentioned in Chapter 3, clay shrinks as it dries. You can prove this to yourself—and in the process check the shrinkage rate of the clay you are using—by cutting a piece of clay slab ¼″ x 1″ x 10″ long. Let it dry thoroughly, then measure its length again. You will probably find that it has shrunk to about 9½″ in length.

The shrinking of clay as it dries presents a problem for the potter. If you just expose a moist clay pot to the air, the surface of it will dry while the inside of the clay is still wet; also the thinner parts will dry faster than the thicker. Uneven drying obviously produces uneven shrinking. As a result, the pot warps out of shape; it may develop cracks or even break to pieces.

The Right Way

The way to avoid warping and cracking is to dry the pot very slowly. In this way you don't get premature drying of surfaces and thin sections; all parts of the clay are just about at the same degree of moisture all the time; all parts shrink at the same rate and so, though the pot is reduced somewhat in size, yet it retains its proportions and shape, and remains firmly in one piece.

THE FIRST STAGE

The newly-modeled pot is standing on a piece of newspaper, or a paper towel, on the bat. Get a sheet of thin plastic and drive the tines of a table fork through it three times, spacing the holes several inches apart. (For drying the pot in the hammock method, similarly pierce three sets of fork-holes in the plastic sheet you put over the carton.) Cover the pot with plastic, tucking it carefully under the edges of the bat, so that there can be no air circulation except through the fork-holes. This will control the rate of drying. Now leave it alone, and try to curb your impatience; the more slowly it dries, the stronger it will be.

LEATHER-HARD

For the next stage, you have to wait till the clay reaches the condition called "leather-hard." A small, thin pot, with a lot of grog in the clay, might get leather-hard in 24 hours. (Because it is porous, the grog helps to speed drying.) A bigger piece might take three, four or more days. At this leather-hard stage, about half the mechanical water has evaporated, so the clay has firmed up considerably.

To test it, remove the plastic and touch the pot. Leather-hard clay should feel cool and slightly damp; it is firm enough that it will not yield to a gentle squeeze of thumb and finger, but it will yield to the pressure of a finger-nail. (Wet the indentation and smooth it over to remove the mark.)

Drying pots. Left: the small pinch-formed pot standing on a bat is covered with sheet plastic. Right: a pot drying in the hammock; notice how the entire hammock structure is covered with plastic.

If the clay is leather-hard, you can now lift the pot and it will hold its shape.

Now is the time to put in a signature, initials, or any other marks you want on the pot; you can inscribe them with a knitting needle, a nail, or any such sharp object.

This is also the time for using certain decorative techniques that will improve the appearance of the pot.

Burnishing

Burnishing involves polishing the surface of the pot with some smooth, rounded object; a teaspoon is good to use, so is a smooth, water-polished pebble; some potters burnish with their thumbs. Burnishing is a good technique if you don't want to glaze the pot; it produces a shiny surface in one firing. However, burnishing does not make a waterproof surface, so it's not adequate for pots that are to hold liquids.

Use short, back-and-forth strokes; you will see at once just how much pressure is required to produce the shiny effect. Support the pot inside with one hand at the point where you are applying the burnishing tool to the outside.

Other Processes

There are several other processess that can best be done at the leather-hard stage.

1. Applying engobe, all over, or in a design.
2. Carving and cutting incised patterns.
3. Boring holes.
4. Joining sections of a pot together, sticking on handles, feet, etc., using slip for adhesive.

Detailed instructions for all these processes are given elsewhere; but it's important to remember that the leather-hard stage is just about your last chance to work on a pot; beyond that, there's little scope for making alterations or improvements.

FINAL DRYING

Now you can take the plastic off and leave the leather-hard pot uncovered to finish drying *in a cool place.* A cool basement is ideal, but otherwise choose the coolest corner of the room, not near a radiator or other heat source, and not in direct sunlight. If you can't provide such a cool place, it's safer to replace the plastic and leave it loosely covering the pot (not tucked in under the bat) till drying is complete.

The final stage of drying may take another 5 to 10 days. The test for completion of drying is that the pot no longer feels cold to the touch. (Moist clay always feels cool.) Once the pot has reached this stage, you can leave it as long as you like before firing; but it must be handled gently, because it's brittle and can easily be chipped or broken.

Grinding

To level uneven spots on the top or bottom of fully-dried greenware, put a few drops of water on a smooth, hard surface—a sheet of glass, a board, a counter-top. Put the rim or foot of the pot flat on the surface and rub it briskly, in a circular motion, for 3 or 4 seconds. That rapidly smooths it off. Finish by a quick wipe with a damp sponge; that slightly rounds off any sharp edges produced by the grinding.

Sanding

To remove small lumps, or to smooth rough areas on curved surfaces of a fully-dried pot, rub with fine sandpaper. Don't put the sandpaper over a block, but hold it in your hand so that it accommodates itself to the curve of the surface you are working on.

I mentioned in Chapter 4 a reason for avoiding sharp edges and corners on pottery (glaze won't adhere to them). So at this stage, after drying is complete, if you find any edges or corners still too sharp, round them off by a light rubbing with sandpaper.

Warning

When grinding or sanding an unfired pot, hold it near the bottom, where the thickness of the base gives it the greatest strength. If you grip it near the top, you may break it, because it's still quite fragile.

6

Firing

EVERY potter should understand the firing process which turns a piece of greenware (unfired pottery), so fragile that it will crumble at one sharp knock, so water-absorbent that it would dissolve in a rainstorm, into a pot that, with reasonable care, will last thousands of years.

FINAL DRYING

In Chapter 5, I emphasized the need for thorough drying of your greenware. Under some circumstances, there may be a doubt as to whether this drying is complete. Perhaps you had to skimp the drying period a bit. Or perhaps there's a very high atmospheric humidity at the time; and the pot obviously cannot get any drier than the air that surrounds it. If there is as little as 2 percent or 3 percent of mechanical water remaining, that's enough to make the pot explode if it is too quickly heated past the boiling point of water.

So, if you have the slightest suspicion that drying may be incomplete, take this precaution: put the greenware in your kitchen oven, set the heat at 66°C. (150°F.) and leave the pots in for about 2 hours.

BISCUIT FIRING & GLAZE FIRING

The initial firing process where the air-dried pots are put once through the kiln is called "Biscuit Firing." Some potters prefer the French word "Bisque" (pronounced "bisk"). This produces an unglazed pot (except for small items made of Egyptian paste, which are glazed on first firing).

Then, where a waterproof or shiny surface is required, you apply glaze materials to a pot that has already been biscuit fired, and fire it again, to melt the glaze and make it adhere firmly to the pot. This second firing is called the "Glaze Firing" and is done at a higher temperature than the biscuit firing.

CUSTOM FIRING

I would suggest that, for a start, you don't try to do your own firing. Concentrate for a while on making the pots; if you find you enjoy the craft and want to continue with it, that will be the time to invest in a kiln.

Most ceramic supply stores do custom firing; so do night schools, community centers, and community colleges that offer ceramics classes. Fees vary with the size of the pot, but are not high. At the time of writing, a piece 8″ x 8″ could be fired for about $1: that's for the biscuit firing, which is all you need for many projects. Glaze firing would probably cost about 50 percent more, because of the higher temperature required, and the need to space the pieces out. (In biscuit firing, the greenware can be stacked up; for glaze firing the pieces must not be allowed to touch, or they will stick together.)

Here are some hints on getting best value from custom firing facilities:

1. Transportation.

To take greenware for firing, pack the pieces in a carton with cloth, or crumpled paper around them to avoid breakage. Unfired clay is not excessively fragile—it will stand a reasonable amount of handling—but all the same, you don't want to let it get knocked about.

2. Biscuit firing.

Tell the kiln operators what clay you have used; they will know what temperature to apply.

3. Glaze firing.

If you know you are going to glaze a pot, it's a good idea to discuss the project with the kiln operator when you pick it up after the biscuit firing. He may be able to offer useful suggestions; he knows what glazes will fire best in the type of kiln being used. In any case, when you bring pots in for glaze firing, you should certainly mention the kind of clay they are made of, and the type of glaze you have used.

YOUR OWN KILN

I unhesitatingly recommend that you get an electric kiln. Gas and oil fired kilns are good for big-scale commercial or school firing, but are just not suitable for home use.

By far the most convenient is the type of kiln that runs off the ordinary household 110-volt electricity supply. If you get a bigger kiln, requiring a 220-volt outlet, you may be faced with the expense of extra wiring for your home.

The kiln I use myself has two separately-wired heating sections; each one plugs into its own 110-volt socket, so either can be used separately, or both at once. The kiln also has 4 risers, by addition or removal of which I can make the kiln higher or lower as required. (Obviously, it's wasteful to heat up more space than is needed.)

Most small kilns are top-loading (i.e. you open them by raising a lid on top). Each kiln should have a small spy-hole in the side; through this spy-hole you can check how the firing process is going, and tell when to turn off the heat.

You will probably see, at stores and schools, front-loading kilns; these are nearly always big ones—too big for your purpose.

A lamp, a covered jar and two small pinch-formed bowls in the kiln. A riser is being added, to give enough height. The inside dimensions of this kiln are a hexagon 6½″ on each side.

Putting on the lid. The peephole is in the front center of the kiln. The kiln is set on a raised base to keep it up off the floor; this must always be used.

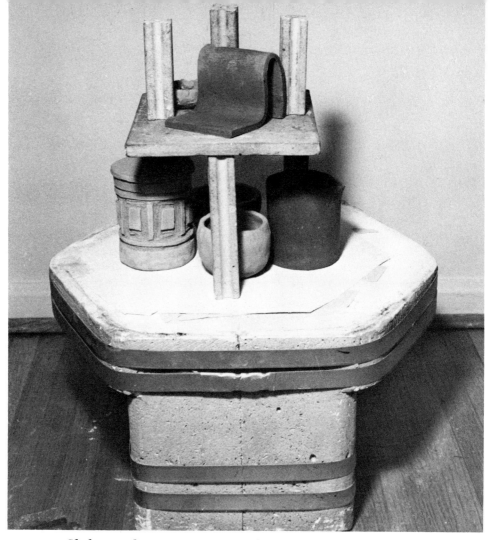

Shelves and posts in use to stack up greenware in the kiln for biscuit firing. For the actual firing, of course, heating elements, risers and lid would be added.

Kiln Furniture

Kiln furniture is an assortment of stands, blocks, and shelves made of special heat-resistant clay or metal; it is used for stacking up pots, to get full use of your kiln capacity, or to keep them from sticking together in glaze firing.

For a start, you might get two shelves, the right size to fit in your kiln, and 9 posts or blocks, 3 of them 2″, 3 of them 4″ and 3 of them 6″

high. I suggest three of each height because it is easier to get a shelf standing level and firm on three blocks than on four; also it saves the space that a fourth block would waste. (Posts are available in many heights, but there's no need to get more than three kinds for a start.)

For glaze firing, it's good to have a few of the 3-pointed stilts (some potters call them pins). If you have an article that is glazed on both sides, stand it on a stilt for the glaze firing in order to keep it up in the air. The glaze then does not stick to the kiln floor or shelf; the only blemishes on the glaze are three tiny spots where it touched the points of the stilt. Stilts come in a range of sizes numbered from 1 to 8, in dimensions from 1″ to 3″ across. Some are made of heat-resistant fireclay. Another kind of stilt is made of nichrome wire; these cost a little more, but have finer points, and so leave smaller marks on the finished pot.

Here's a trick to avoid using a needlessly high post, and so wasting kiln space. Suppose you are about to fire a dish 2¼″ high. Use the 2″ posts, but put a little lump of clay on top of each, and raise the shelf just high enough to clear the dish.

BISCUIT FIRING: THE TWO STAGES

It's well to realize that there are *two* stages. Although it's the second stage that produces the major visible changes in your pot, the first is essential, and must not be rushed or skimped.

Stage 1

The first stage consists of slowly raising the temperature to drive off the combined water from the clay. This change begins at about 220°C. and is completed by about 700°C., that is by the time the pot is red-hot.

I would emphasize that the temperature increase at this stage *must be slow*. Otherwise, if you try to rush the firing, the chemical water will be driven off too fast, and it will make the pot explode. A precaution I always use is to plug in only one of the two heating circuits, and leave the lid off the kiln for half an hour. Close the lid, let the temperature rise for 2 hours, then plug in the second circuit.

Stage 2

Above 850°C. begins the process of vitrification: some of the clay ingredients melt and form glass which, on cooling, will hold the whole pot firmly together. The risk here is that if you let the temperature rise too high, there will be too much vitrification, and your pot will simply collapse into a molten blob on the floor of the kiln.

Each type of clay has a certain "vitrification range," that is a temperature range between the point where vitrification starts, and where the clay melts. Obviously, the narrower that range is, the more exact temperature control is required, and the more difficult it becomes to fire pots satisfactorily. The type of clay that I am recommending here has a fairly wide vitrification range; so, with a reasonable degree of care, you should have no problems with over-firing.

(Whoever you buy a kiln from will give you operating instructions for that particular model.)

TEMPERATURE CONTROL

Then how are you to tell when the temperature has reached vitrification point? Ordinary thermometers are useless at these high temperatures. Through the spy-hole you can look into the kiln, but when the whole interior gets red hot, you can't see the pots.

The easiest, cheapest way to control kiln temperature is with pyrometric cones. These are slender cones made of special types of clay; each one melts at a fixed temperature. The cone is mounted in a clay base, standing with just a slight tilt.

There are forty or more different cones made, covering a range from 585°C. (1085°F.) to 1595°C. (2903°F.). We don't need to bother with all of these. Here is a list of cones to cover the firing range of projects described in this book.

Cone Number	Melts at	Temperature
010	895°C.	1643°F.
09	930°C.	1706°F.
08	950°C.	1742°F.
07	990°C.	1814°F.
06	1015°C.	1859°F.
05	1040°C.	1904°F.
04	1060°C.	1940°F.

You can buy cones by the dozen or, more cheaply, in boxes of fifty. Here's how you use them. The modeling clay that I've recommended in this book generally requires, for biscuit firing, the temperature indicated by cone 06.

So get one cone 07 and one 06. Take a ¾ inch ball of clay and flatten it out (this is called a cone pat); stick the cones in the cone pat with the numbers towards your spy-hole, and slightly tilted. The tilt should be arranged so that, when the cones melt, they will fall away from the heating element, and will not touch any of the pieces being fired.

Start up the kiln; allow the preliminary warming as described above, then close the lid and apply full heat. From time to time, glance through the spy-hole, looking particularly at cone number 07. (By the way, keep the spy-hole plugged with a conical lump of clay except when you're looking

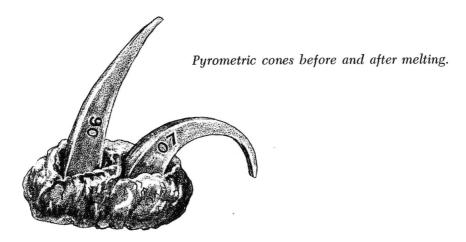

Pyrometric cones before and after melting.

through it. The wider end of the lump is outside, so it can't fall in.) So long as cone 07 is standing up straight, you know the kiln is not nearly at the required temperature. When 07 melts and falls down, keep close watch. When the tip of 06 just begins to bend over, that's the proper temperature, so you shut off the heat.

COOLING

Once the heat is turned off, leave the kiln to cool *slowly*. Control your impatience: don't open the lid prematurely to take a look at the finished pots. If you do that, the rush of cool air is likely to crack or break them. For safety, many potters let their kilns cool overnight.

GLAZE FIRING

Most of the glazes described in this book can be fired at cone 04. So for this purpose, you would mount cones 05 and 04 in your cone pat. Warm up the kiln slowly just as you did for biscuit firing. Look at the cones from time to time. When 05 melts and falls down, that's your first warning. When 04 begins to bend over, turn off the power, and leave the kiln to cool.

LOADING THE KILN

First, here are some general principles for loading. As soon as you get your own kiln, there's natural temptation to pop a pot or two in it, and turn on the heat. Resist that temptation! For economy, it's best to fill the kiln as full as possible for each firing. Here are some hints for making most effective use of kiln space.

   Put heavy pots on the floor of the kiln; then put in posts and a shelf, and lighter pieces on that; if there's room, put in a second shelf for the lightest pieces.

   Put pieces of the same, or nearly the same height on the same level, to get best space-value from your shelves.

Covers and lids should be fired on the boxes or jars they belong to.

If you have a kiln of adjustable capacity, and not enough pots to fill it, then remove one or two risers; there's no sense in heating empty kiln-space.

Don't try to crowd in *too many* pots by jamming them up against the walls; no pot should be nearer than ½″ to a heating element.

Now for some hints on biscuit and glaze firing.

1. Biscuit firing.

If temperature is properly controlled, there is no risk that the pots will stick together; so you can pack them in as closely as you like. Small pots can stand inside bigger ones; or small articles like beads, tiles, etc. can be stacked inside a pot to save space. The only limitation is that all pieces fired together should be made of the same clay.

2. Glaze firing.

Here you cannot let the glazed parts of two pieces touch or, after the glaze melts and solidifies again, they will be firmly stuck together.

Glazed surfaces also will stick to the kiln bottom or shelf; so if you have to fire a piece that is glazed on both sides, put it on a stilt.

Small amounts of molten glaze sometimes drip off the pots during firing. To prevent these from sticking to the kiln bottom and shelves, use a kiln wash. You can get kiln wash at the ceramic supply store; it is a powder to be mixed with water. Prepare it according to directions and paint it on kiln bottom and shelves with a brush before each glaze firing. Then you'll find that any spilled glaze can be easily removed. (There's no need to use kiln wash for biscuit firing.)

FIRING TIMES

When using your own kiln, keep record of the time for each firing; this lets you estimate times for future firings of similar work. At first, you'll have to take frequent looks through the spy-hole at your cones; but after a few firings, you have a fair idea of how long it's going to take, so you know 10 or 15 minutes ahead of time when to start watching the cone.

On a biscuit firing, if you over-fire for 10 or 15 minutes, it won't do much damage; but for glaze firing, you definitely don't want to under-fire or over-fire. And anyway, there's no sense in wasting electricity by over-firing or under-firing. (Under-firing uses the current, but doesn't deliver the finished product!) So careful observation and record-keeping will enable you to get accurate control of your firing operations.

KILN MAINTENANCE

Treat your kiln gently, in moving it, in adding and removing risers, in loading and unloading, in putting on and taking off the lid. The firebrick of which it is made is not nearly so strong as building brick, indeed, it is quite soft and fragile. The heating elements, too, can easily be knocked out of place or broken.

If, by accident, you do break a heating section, a riser, or the lid of your kiln, get a replacement part from the same store that sold you the kiln.

Heating elements, in time, burn out. (It's not surprising, considering the great heat they generate.) You can get replacements. Tell the storekeeper what you want them for; tell him the inside circumference of the kiln, and what temperature you want to fire at. (If you're firing to cone 04, be on the safe side and say 2,000°F.)

7

Pinch Forming

This is probably the oldest method of forming a pot; it was the traditional method for making Japanese tea-bowls. Pinch forming can still be used to make strong, good-looking pots of various shapes and sizes.

A PINCH-FORMED BOWL

For the first project, take a ball of freshly-wedged clay about 2½" in diameter. Holding it in one hand, drive the thumb of the other hand into it, about half-way through, to make a hollow.

Then begin to make the sides and base thinner, by squeezing the clay between the thumb and finger, working your way round and round, widening and deepening the hole in the middle. After a few rounds, you have a thick-walled, roughly-shaped bowl about 3" across and 3" high.

The next stage is to make the sides still thinner, and give them the final shape. Hold the bowl in the hollow of your left hand (or right hand, if you are left-handed). Begin pinching at the bottom of the sides, and squeeze them down to ⅜ inch; turn the bowl as you work, but keep the pinches close together, so that the surface, inside and out, is fairly smooth.

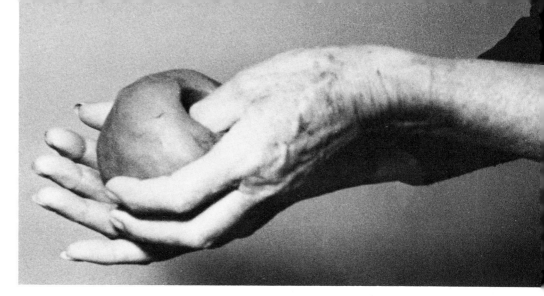

Preliminary stage of pinch forming a small bowl. The thumb has been pressed into the center of the clay ball, and the fingers are beginning to thin out and shape the sides.

Keep pinching like this, round and round, gradually working up the sides. Flare the pot out a little in the middle and in again towards the top. Slightly reduce the thickness of the sides towards the top, down to about ¼″.

To give the bowl a flat base, put it on the board, reach down inside and give a gentle rotary pressure with your fingertips, inside the bottom, to press the clay down smoothly against the board. Lastly, with a damp sponge, smooth of the rim of the bowl.

Here are a couple of hints on this method.

1. Don't spend too much time working on one pot; if you do, the top may dry and split from the warmth of your hands. With a little practice, you can make a bowl of this size in 10 minutes.

2. Don't try to make the pot perfectly slick or exact in shape, like something stamped out of a mold. It will look most effective if it retains something of the free form associated with this method.

The three small pots in the photo were made separately, then stuck together when leather-hard. Roughen the points of contact; apply slip; put finger and thumb inside and squeeze the pots together for a few seconds; they will stick together. Cover them again with plastic,and leave them to dry.

Several pinch-formed bowls. The three at the left were stuck to-gether with slip at the leather-hard stage, then fired and glazed. The bowl in foreground is fully dried, ready for biscuit firing. The one at the right is still drying under plastic. All five are about 4″ across at the widest point.

JEWELRY

Pinch forming is well suited to the making of jewelry—necklaces, pendants, earrings, etc. Egyptian paste is much used for jewelry, but ordinary clay is good, too, left in its natural color, stained or glazed.

Pendant

Take a ball of paste or clay about the size of a walnut and pinch-form it into a suitable shape—pear-shaped, oval, free-form, or whatever you like —about ⅜″ thick at one end, thinning down to about ¼″ at the other. Pierce a hole through the thicker end with a knitting needle.

Cover with plastic and leave till leather-hard, At this stage, you can, if you like, burnish the pendant, apply engobe, carve an incised pattern, or make one or more cut-out sections.

Finish drying, then fire. Egyptian paste will be glazed on the one firing. Ordinary clay can, if you wish, then be glazed and fired again; or you can stain the pieces without a second firing.

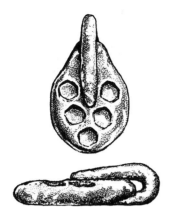

Pendant forms. Note placement of holes for mounting.

Pinch-formed pendants and necklaces. Light necklace, matt Egyptian paste. Dark necklace and pendant, glossy turquoise Egyptian paste. LEFT FRONT: *unglazed clay pendant.* CENTER FRONT: *clay pendant, glazed one side.*

Necklace

With your hands, roll out a cylinder of clay or paste about a foot long. The thickness will depend on the size of beads you want to make; it can be as thin as a cigarette, or as thick as your thumb. Cut the cylinder into equal sections.

Take each section separately and, by rolling and pinching, form it into a bead shape. With a knitting needle or nail pierce a hole through it. Another type of necklace can be made from flat pieces that are not threaded on a string, but linked together. Take balls of clay or paste about ¾″ across; flatten them out, and form them into suitable shapes—round, oval, oblong, or whatever you like—and put away till leather-hard. Then pierce each one with two holes. After firing, the pieces can be linked together with short pieces of chain or wire.

Earrings

Some craft stores sell earring hardware, ready for you to put your own "jewels" on. You can make pieces, to match your pendant or necklace, and mount them on the clips.

Other Jewelry Forms

The projects described above are all quite simple to make—each in one solid piece. Here are some methods that are a little more complex.

Take an egg-sized ball of paste; with your hands, roll it on the board into a long cylinder, somewhat thinner than a cigarette. Cut off a piece about 8″ long, and twine it into one of the shapes shown in the diagram. Where the pieces cross, and where the ends join, carefully pinch them together for strength.

A variant of this technique is to use the rolling pin and slats to make a strip of clay about 8 inches long and ¼″ thick. Then, using one of the slats as a guide, cut off a narrow strip, about ⅜″ wide. Now use this, in the same way as you used the cylinder; but for extra interest, you can twist the strip as you form it.

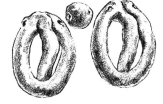

Twined pendant forms.

The twisted strip method.

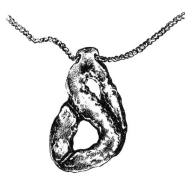

Firing Jewelry

There are no problems in firing jewelry made of unglazed clay, or of the matt-finish Egyptian paste. Simply lay the pieces on the floor or shelf of the kiln; or, to save space put them inside another unglazed pot that is being fired at the same time. Fire to cone 04.

But it requires a little extra care to fire the glossy-finish Egyptian paste, or to do the second firing of glazed clay pieces. The problem is that if such items touch while the glaze is molten, they will stick together. Here are some hints on solving the problem.

1. For flat pendants.

Only one side is going to show when the pendant is in use; so apply the glaze only to the face and lay the pendant on the unglazed side for firing. With the glossy-finished Egyptian paste, you can set the pendant on a stilt for firing. Then there will be just the three tiny marks in the glaze on the reverse side.

2. For beads.

If, in forming the beads, you flatten one or both ends, you can stand them on end for firing, and then the glaze will be spoiled only on one end of each bead, where it won't show after they are strung.

Or you can string the beads on a piece of 10-gauge nichrome (ny-krome) heat-resistant wire suspended between two clay blocks, and then the glaze will be perfect all around. You can buy the wire at ceramic-supply or electric-supply stores. Pendants and other pieces can similarly be strung on the nichrome wire if you have it.

Arrangement of nichrome wire, supporting blocks and beads, for firing.

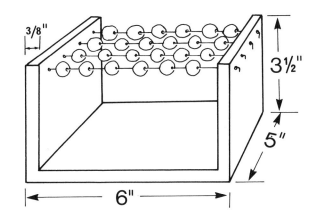

Because of the extra trouble and space-requirements for firing it becomes rather costly to have this glazed jewelry fired commercially. So I would suggest that you begin with unglazed (or matt Egyptian paste) jewelry, and postpone making the glazed pieces until you have a kiln of your own.

CHESS MEN

Some of the well-known patterns of chess men were designed to be carved from wood or ivory; they are not suitable to be formed of clay.

Here is the design for a set that is well adapted to this medium. Made in the size shown, they will suit the board with 1½″ squares described in Chapter 4.

The customary names for the two sets are White and Black, but any two contrasting colors will do, so long as you have 8 pawns, king, queen, 2 bishops, 2 knights, and 2 rooks (castles) in each color.

Here, as with the checker men, you can leave one set in their natural color, and give the other set 3 coats of black engobe when leather-hard. Complete drying, and fire to cone 04.

There is no need to glaze the chess men, unless you particularly want to do so. A good finish is provided by rubbing the biscuit-fired pieces with several coats of wax floor or shoe polish. (You can, if you like, use brown polish for the "white" men, and black for the black.) This gives them a glossy finish and—equally important for such a purpose—gives them a nice feel under the frequent handling they will get during play.

Design for chess men.

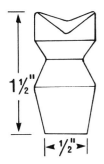

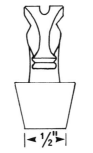
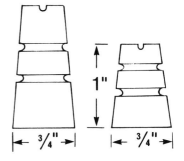

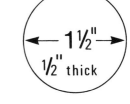

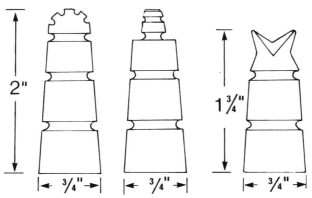

8

Coil and Strip Forming

THE two rather similar techniques described in this chapter are exceedingly flexible; with coils, or with strips, you can form shallow bowls, deep bowls, straight-sided vases, narrow-necked vases, table lamps, planters, and so on.

COIL FORMING

The simplest shape to produce by coil forming is a straight-sided cylinder; so I suggest you begin by making a coffee mug.

Cover a bat with paper. On it put a lump of clay about 2″ in diameter and with your hand pat it into a flat slab ⅜″ thick. From this slab, cut out a circle 3¼″ in diameter. (You can use a cardboard template, or mark the circle directly on the clay with a pair of dividers.) This circle will be the base of the mug. Near the outer edge of the circle, scratch out a groove about ⅛″ deep, with the wire-loop tool.

Now take a slightly bigger ball of clay; squeeze it into a cigar shape; then put it on a smooth board and roll it back and forth with your hands, making it longer and thinner. Keep the board slightly damp, by sprinkling a little water on it with your fingers, to prevent the clay from drying out as you work. Keep rolling the clay till you have a long cylinder, ⅜″ in diameter. Try to make it perfectly smooth and even, like a long pencil.

Rolling out a length of coil. The small bowl at left contains water with which the potter can dampen her hands when necessary. At lower left is the base of a pot, ready for application of the coil.

Break off, by twisting, a piece of this cylinder about 10″ long. Coil it around the outside edge of the base, so that it sits neatly in the groove. Press the two ends together, and join them well by smoothing the clay back and forth with your fingers, till there is no trace of the joint.

Applying the first coil to the base of a pot. Note how it fits into the groove prepared to receive it. The small bowl contains slip, to be applied with the paint brush when affixing handles to mugs, knobs to lids, etc. The spare length of coil is kept covered with plastic, so that it does not dry out.

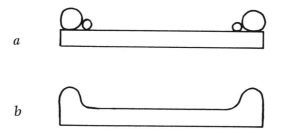

a

b

(a) Joint and coil before the cylinder is worked in.
(b) Cylinder worked in to strengthen the joint.

With downward pressure of your fingertips, work the inside of the coil well into the base. Similarly weld the outside of the coil to the outer edge of the base.

To strengthen the joint between base and sides, roll out with your hands a cylinder ⅛″ thick. Lay this around inside the joint, overlapping its ends ¼″ and welding them together.

With the small wooden modeling tool, or a teaspoon handle, work the cylinder into the angle, so that base and side are welded into a smooth, rounded joint. Support the outside with your fingers as you apply the pressure within.

The wooden tool is being used to weld the first coil firmly to the base of the pot.

Make another coil the same size as the first. Dampen the top of the first coil with a sponge, and lay the second coil squarely on top of it. Join the ends tightly together. Smooth the coil downward, both inside and out, to join it firmly to the first one.

Keep adding coils until the sides of the mug stand 3¾″ high. Try to get the sides fairly straight, but don't worry about making the mug look as if it had been stamped out by a machine.

If you find that you've left a bad bulge somewhere, support the inside of the mug with your fingers, and gently slap the outside with a paddle to push it into shape.

On some coil-formed pots, it looks effective to leave the finger-marks on the sides: they form an interesting pattern. But for a mug, it's better to smooth off the surface. So take a small, damp sponge and, supporting the outside with your fingers, smooth off any rough spots inside, moving the sponge with a round-and-round polishing motion. Then, supporting the inside, similarly smooth off the outside. Finish by smoothing the rim with the sponge.

Now, for the handle, make a roll of clay ⅜″ thick. Cut off a piece 5½″ long, and shape it to the form shown on the diagram. Lay it on the bat beside the mug, cover both with plastic, and set aside till they are leather-hard.

Shape of handle for the mug.

Cutting the recess in the base of a leather-hard jug.

Now you can cut a recess in the bottom of the mug, so that it will stand firmly, even on a slightly uneven surface. Turn the mug upside-down, take the wire-loop modeling tool and cut out the middle of the base to a depth of ⅛″ (no more!). Leave a rim ¼″ wide all around.

After the cutting is done, smooth the recess with a modeling tool or spoon handle.

Now turn the mug right-side up; roughen the ends of the handle, and the spots where you want the handle to adhere to the mug; apply a little slip and press the handle into place. Hold it there with one hand, and with the point of the modeling tool, weld the handle and mug together, all around the points of contact.

At this stage, with all tableware, it's a good idea to make sure that it stands level. A mug, plate, or bowl that rocks on its base always seems to indicate poor workmanship. If you find that the mug doesn't stand level, flatten the base by grinding or sanding, as described in Chapter 5.

Now is the time for adding a decorative pattern in engobe, if you wish to do so. Then leave the mug until it is fully dried. Give it a biscuit firing to cone 06; then apply a clear, non-lead glaze and give the glaze firing to cone 04.

More Coil-Formed Projects

Here are some more projects to make with this technique. For all such pots, follow the same basic procedure as you did for the coffee mug. Weld the base and the first coil firmly together. To help maintain an accurate shape, it's a good idea to make a cardboard template to fit the curves of the pot.

If you have in your home, or see in a friend's home, or in a book, a pot with a shape that particularly pleases you, then make a template, full-size, and use it to guide you in making a pot in the same design.

In planning coil-formed pots, you can follow these general rules. A ¼″ coil is strong enough for pots up to 5″ high; for pots 5″ to 8″ high, use ⅜″ coils; for pots 8″ to 12″ high, use ½″ coils. Whatever the size of the pot, cut the coil after each completed round, leaving ¼″ extra to weld the two ends together with your fingers.

(By the way, except for small items like mugs, if you want to make cylindrical forms, it's easier to use the mold-forming methods described in Chapter 9.)

A wide-mouthed bowl with flared sides.

Template for a vase with neck as wide as base and well-curved sides.

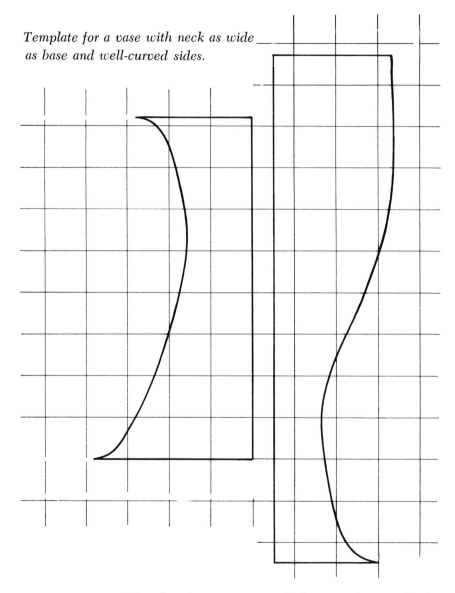

Template for a narrow-necked vase with curved sides.

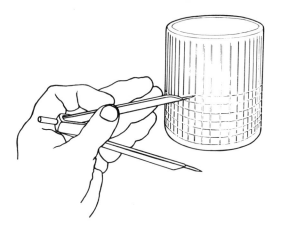

Using dividers to measure height for a horizontal line. Vertical lines are already incised on the pot.

Checking the contour of a vase with the template.

Finishing Coil-Formed Pots

The process described above gives you the basic shape of the pot; here are some ideas for finishing it off.

1. Simply leave the finger-marks on the outside; for a different color, you can apply stain or glaze after the biscuit firing.

2. For a smooth finish, paddle or burnish the surface.

3. Create an incised pattern on the outer surface, at the leather-hard stage. Here's one way to get the pattern looking fairly regular.

Use a narrow wire modeling tool or a bobby pin. Hold a ruler straight up and down against the side of the pot; draw the tool down it, so that it gouges out a vertical line. Cut a series of these vertical lines around the pot, not too wide apart. When you come to the last inch or two, judge the spacing of the last few lines to make them fairly even. (There's no need for machine-like exactitude.)

To make horizontal lines, measure up from the table, and make a series of little marks all around. A pair of dividers will do this job very well. Then use these marks to guide the tool in cutting the horizontal line.

The effect of any incised or raised design features can be heightened by suitable use of color. With engobe at the leather-hard stage, or with different colored glazes on the second firing, you can emphasize the raised or depressed design elements.

LEFT: *a coil-formed pot 10″ high, 5″ wide, carved with a deeply incised pattern, and glazed.* RIGHT: *a coil-formed figure, 16″ high. It is a hollow structure, built in much the same way as a pot; pieces are added for arms, costume, details, as the construction proceeds. The features are painted on with manganese, red iron and water; then the figure is finished with several different-colored glazes. This is a very advanced example of coil-forming.* FOREGROUND: *three small pots, oval in cross-section; the largest is approximately 3½″ x 1½″, with sides 4½″ high. The method is to make the oval base first, then cut out a single slab for the sides, wrap it around, weld it firmly to the base, and weld the ends of the slab together.*

STRIP FORMING

The principle of this technique is the same as that of coil forming but, for making smooth-sided pots, it is quicker. You roll out a slab of clay ¼″ thick and cut from it a series of strips, each 1″ wide and ¼″ longer than is needed to go once around the pot. Then you apply these strips very much as you did the coils: stand the strip on edge; weld the ends together, and weld its lower edge to the strip below. For bigger projects, the strips can be ⅜″ or ½″ thick, to give more strength to the sides of the pot, and up to 1½″ wide.

PLANTER

Roll out or press out a slab of clay ½″ thick, and from it cut out the base to the shape shown below.

Now roll out a slab ¼″ thick, and from it cut a strip 1″ wide. With a comb or hacksaw blade, roughen all around the base, ½″ in from edge; with brush or finger, apply a thin layer of slip. Stand the 1″ strip on edge, on this roughened part; weld it to the base, by finger-pressure, as you go, so that it stands up by itself. Cut the strip so that its ends overlap by about ¼″ and weld the two ends together by pressure between finger and thumb. Strengthen the joint between base and strip by working into the angle a ⅛″ cylinder just as I described for the coil-formed mug.

Planter, 5″ x 8″ x 4″ high, with rounded corners.

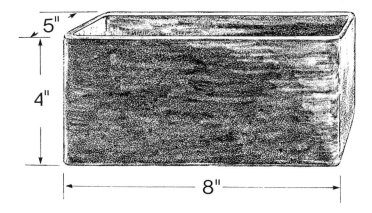

Now cut out another 1″ x ¼″ strip. Roughen the upper ¼″ of the first strip, and paint the roughened part with slip. Now join on the second strip, making it overlap the first one by about ¼″ (rather like wooden siding on the wall of a house) all the way around. At first, press it into place with finger and thumb just enough to hold it up. Weld the ends together.

Now work around to smooth and strengthen the joint. Put your thumb outside and forefinger inside. Slide the thumb downward so that it moves clay from the second strip downward to the first. At the same time, slide the forefinger upward, so that it moves clay from the first strip up to weld on to the second. Continue this thumb-and-finger welding right around till the whole joint is firm and smooth.

Keep adding more strips until the sides are 4″ high. I suggested cutting each strip in one piece, but if you prefer to work with shorter strips, you can build each layer in two or three pieces. Simply overlap the pieces ¼″ and work the two ends together with thumb and finger until they are smooth.

Watch the shape of the sides. If you find you have made a bulge, you can restore the correct shape by paddling, as described under coil forming.

CANDY BOX

Here's a circular candy box of which the side consists of a single strip.

The base is a circular slab 8″ in diameter and ⅜″ thick. The side is a single strip, 1½″ wide, 25½″ long, ⅜″ thick. (If you find this long strip too hard to handle, you can make it in two parts, attach each separately, then weld them together.)

Set up the side as previously described, strengthening the joint with a ⅛″ cylinder worked into the angle between base and side.

For the lid, make a circle 8½″ in diameter and ⅜″ thick. Make the knob for the lid, but don't attach it yet.

Cover the box, lid and knob, and leave them till they are leather-hard.

This strip-formed table lamp was made in two sections. The upper part is 17" high; the base, a small bowl, 7" wide and 2" deep, is fired separately, inverted, and glued to the main part. The surface texture was obtained by scratching with a knitting needle while the clay was leather-hard.

Strip-formed candy box.

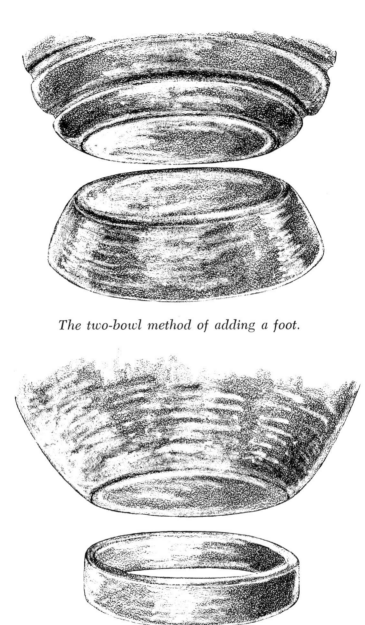

The two-bowl method of adding a foot.

The circle method of adding a foot.

Now carve the design in the lid with the bobby-pin tool. Make a strip of clay ¼″ x ¼″, and stick it around the under side of the lid, far enough in from the edge so that it will fit inside the walls of the box, and form a rim to prevent the lid slipping off. Stick the knob in position at the center of the lid with slip.

Put the lid carefully in place on the box. Cover the whole thing with plastic and leave it to dry with the lid in position; lid and box will then shrink together, and will be a good fit.

NOTES ON STRIP FORMING

Shapes. Note that strip-formed pots need not be restricted to round or square shapes. The photograph illustrates a three-cornered shape that is effective in this technique.

Big pieces. For making large pots, it's advisable to leave the first strip uncovered for 20 minutes or so to firm up, so that it will support the weight of the next.

Adding a foot. Here are two methods for adding a foot to a bowl or dish:

1. Simply make another bowl, smaller in diameter, and quite shallow —say about 1″ deep. Leave them till they are leather-hard; then roughen the bases and stick them together with slip; the smaller bowl, upside-down, forms a foot for the bigger.

2. Roll out a strip as wide as you want the foot to be high (¾″ inch or 1 inch are useful heights). Form a circle the diameter of the foot you want. Overlap and weld the ends together. Leave circle and bowl till they are leather-hard, then roughen the contact area, and stick them together with slip.

Adding stoppers. To make a stopper for a narrow-necked bottle, mold the stopper to the shape required, with its outer dimension equal to the inside of the bottle neck. Carve the knob when leather-hard. If, when the stopper is fully dried, it does not fit properly, use sandpaper to make it fit.

Note. An important point concerning stoppers: glaze is applied only on the upper part. The portion that fits inside the neck is left unglazed.

Three-sided vase. The vase is 15″ high; the neck is a triangle 1½″ on each side; at the widest part, the triangle is 6½″ on each side.

Three coil-formed bottles. LEFT: 12″ high; copper oxide was painted in the carved pattern before firing, to produce the dark color; green glaze. CENTER: 16″ high; not glazed; antique gold finish. RIGHT: 12″ high; deep turquoise glaze. All three bottles were carved with the bobby-pin tool.

9

Mold Forming

WITH a mold and some clay you can, if you wish, produce half a dozen or a dozen identical bowls, cups, or platters. On the other hand, you can produce, from the same mold, several pieces that are *not* identical!

VARIABLE TEXTURE

Get a shallow bowl about 5″ to 6″ across and line it with cloth, stretched to lie smooth. This is your mold.

Make a lot of clay balls, ½″ in diameter. Press them together in a single layer, around the inside of the mold; but *don't* press the clay so hard against the mold as to flatten the balls completely. The aim is to leave a pebbled texture on the outside of the bowl when it is finished.

Smooth the inside of the newly-formed clay bowl with a modeling tool, or with your thumb. (I find the thumb is really the most useful of tools for smoothing—better than anything of wood or metal!)

A bowl like this will need feet if it's to stand firm. Make three or four clay balls, ¾″ across; flatten them slightly. Put them beside the bowl, cover the whole thing with plastic and set it aside to dry. When the bowl is leather-hard, take it out of the mold; you'll find that the cloth comes away easily at this stage.

Now roughen one flattened side of each of the balls; roughen the spots on the pot where you wish them to go, and stick them on with slip. Now leave the bowl to finish drying in the usual way.

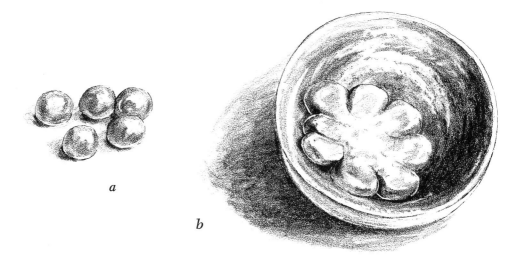

a

b

(a) Balls of clay ready for mold forming. (b) Starting to form the bowl in the mold. (c) Pebbled texture produced by mold form.

c

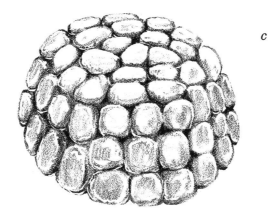

For finishing a bowl like this, one good method is to glaze the inside and stain the outside: if carefully done, this staining will heighten the effect of the pebbled texture. (For details of staining, see Chapter 10.)

Here are three ways in which you can get a range of different textures from the same mold, and the same process.

1. Use bigger or smaller balls of clay.

2. Apply more or less pressure when putting the clay balls into the mold.

3. Use a heavily-textured fabric, such as burlap, to line the mold.

Inside of a bowl formed by this method. After the biscuit firing, a dark green glaze was applied; when the glaze was dry, manganese powder was sprinkled on, very lightly, to give a black speckled effect.

Outside of the same bowl. This shows the texture produced by ball forming. It was not glazed, but a dark walnut stain was applied. Felt pads were stuck on the ball feet.

Inside mold forming. The mold has been lined with cloth, and the clay slab shaped inside it, and cut to size. The inside, and edge of the newly-formed bowl are now being smoothed with a sponge.

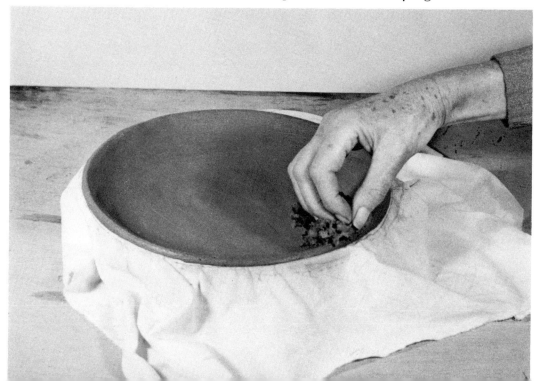

Leave the bowl exposed to the air till it is firm, but not leather-hard (this will take from 2 to 5 hours, depending on how moist the clay is). Then turn the bowl over on to a bat, as shown. The original bowl used as a mold is now visible on top of the cloth.

The mold has been removed, and the cloth is being peeled off.

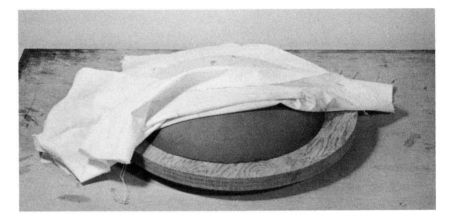

To add a base, take a strip 1″ wide, form it into a circle and weld it by finger and tool to the bottom of the bowl. A small coil is added and worked into the joint between base and bowl, for extra strength. Now, to give the base time to harden, leave it exposed till it is firm; meanwhile, keep the rim of the bowl soft by laying a strip of damp cloth around in contact with it.

To deepen the bowl, cut a strip of clay 1¼″ wide, and weld it to the rim. For convenience in working, it is best to add the strip in two sections.

Welding the inside of the strip to the rim. Here again, a small coil has been added and is being worked into the joint, for extra strength.

Adding the second half of the strip. Note how the knife is used to cut the strip to the exact length for a close fit.

The finished bowl, before decoration. This illustrates how the shape derived from the original mold can be modified to suit your requirements.

Making an incised design with a fork in the finished bowl.

MORE INSIDE MOLD PROJECTS

After completing the bowl described above, you can go on to make larger bowls by the same method.

Use a large plate as mold, lined with cloth. The resulting plate will need a base; so cut a long strip of clay ¼″ x ¼″ and stick it on the underside of the leather-hard plate, in a circle, about 2 inches in from the rim.

The top of the plate can be decorated with an engobe or incised pattern. (If the plate is to be used for food-service remember to use a non-lead glaze!)

A shallow cake-tin serves well as a mold; lined with clay, it will produce a planter. For a rectangular tin, you'll find difficulty in lining it smoothly with cloth. So instead, grease the inside of the tin, and line it with paper cut to shape so that it fits without wrinkling. The grease makes the paper stick to the tin while you apply the clay.

OUTSIDE MOLD FORMING

The pots described above are made inside a mold. But a wide range of projects can be made by forming clay *outside* a mold (much like putting a plaster cast outside an arm or leg). Here are some examples.

ROCK MOLD

Find a rounded rock about 5″ to 8″ across. A water-smoothed rock from sea or lake shore, or from a river bed, is ideal. Don't bother searching for a piece that is symmetrical; a somewhat irregular shape will be more interesting.

Put the rock on the board and cover it with a piece of net or cheesecloth, pulled taut and smooth. If necessary to keep the rock steady while you work, push three or four small balls of clay between it and the board.

Now to apply the clay, break off walnut-sized pieces, press them on, and smooth them out with your thumb, welding them firmly together, till you have the rock covered.

This is the rough shape of your bowl, lying upside-down over the rock mold. Now you want to make feet for it, so that it will stand steady. Make three balls of clay, about ¾″ across; place them near the top of the bowl (i.e. near what is the top now, but what will be the bottom when it's turned over). Weld the feet firmly to the surface of the bowl with a modeling tool.

Drying

Now here's an important technical point. With the inside mold forming process described earlier in this chapter, you can leave the pot in the mold to dry; as the clay shrinks, it pulls clear of the mold. But for outside mold forming, you must remove the pot from the mold before it gets too dry; otherwise, as the clay shrinks, the mold does not yield, and the pot cracks to pieces.

So here's the procedure. After attaching the feet, let the pot stand 20 minutes uncovered for the clay to stiffen up somewhat.

Now pick up the whole thing—rock, cloth and roughly-formed bowl—turn it over and put it down on a bat.

With an old-fashioned hatpin or a long needle, cut off excess clay in a straight line all around the rock. You must not cut above the widest part of the rock, or you won't be able to get the rock out later; but by cutting at or below the widest part, you have considerable scope to vary the depth of the finished bowl. To guide you in cutting a straight level line for the rim, you can use a pair of dividers to make a series of marks all around, at a uniform height above the bat; or you can steady the needle against a wooden block as you move it around.

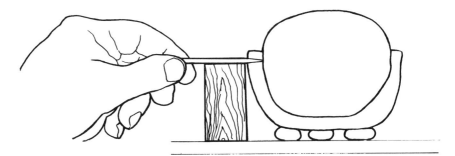

Using a wooden block to support the needle in cutting rim.

Different-shaped bowls, shallow, medium and deep, from one rounded rock.

Lift out the rock, cover the bowl with plastic, and leave it to dry till leather-hard. Then you can remove the cloth, and do any further processing that is appropriate at this stage—burnishing the inside of the bowl, for example. Cover the bowl with plastic again, and finish drying in the usual way. With the typical rounded rock, you can get several markedly different shapes of bowls, by using different parts of the rock as your mold.

MORE OUTSIDE MOLDED PROJECTS

This simple method is very versatile; you can use various cans, jars, and bottles as molds for outside forming of candy jars, cigarette jars, cookie jars, beer mugs, cream jugs, etc.

Various cylindrical molds. CENTER FRONT: *Cut-down plastic bleach container.* LEFT REAR: *orange-juice concentrate can.* CENTER REAR: *section of cardboard tube on which carpet was rolled.* RIGHT REAR: *whisky bottle carton covered with newspaper.*

A mug being formed on mold. The bottom has been partly welded to the sides; seam in side is being welded by finger pressure.

A group of projects, all formed on molds and glazed. Lamp: 8" high, 5½" diameter. Tall vase: the design was incised with the bobby-pin tool. Covered jar: the incised design was painted with copper oxide before the biscuit firing, to produce the dark lines after firing. The vase at right was lightly antiqued with gold after the glaze firing.

For straight-sided pieces, a convenient procedure is to cover the mold with newspaper, held in place by cellulose tape. Roll out a sheet of clay for the bottom, cut it to shape and set it in place. Roll out a sheet that will make the sides, cut it to shape, weld it firmly to the bottom, and overlap and weld the vertical joint.

Let the pot firm up for about 20 to 30 minutes, depending on its size and thickness, then cut the rim, remove the mold, and proceed with drying in the usual way.

When pulling the pot off a paper-covered mold, it's often easier to pull the paper along with the clay, and then remove the paper from inside the pot.

Three On One

Here's a project for making three different pots—a mug, cream jug, and sugar bowl—on one mold. I used a baking-powder can, of 2⅜″ diameter, but any cylinder about this size will do.

The mug

Roll out a slab ¼″ thick; from it cut a circle 3⅜″ across for the base and a rectangle 9½″ x 3½″ for the sides. Form the cylindrical body of the mug around the mold; weld the base on to it with your thumb. Use a sponge to smooth off finger-marks. Give it about 20 minutes to firm up, then slide it off the mold.

Meanwhile, for the handle, roll out a cylinder 5/16″ thick, cut off a piece 5″ long and form it into the C shape shown in the diagram.

Shape of handle for mug & cream jug.

Cover mug and handle with plastic, and leave them till they are leather-hard.

Check that the ends of the handle will fit flush on the side of the mug; if necessary, trim them with a knife so that they do. Roughen the handle-ends and the spots on the mug where it is to touch; apply slip, press the handle in place, and weld it there with firm thumb pressure all around the points of contact.

Finish drying; fire to cone 06; then apply a leadless glaze and fire again to cone 04.

The cream jug

Form this just like the mug except that, after you take it off the mold, shape the spout as shown in the photograph. To make a clean-pouring jug, after you have formed it, pull the lip of the spout up a little; if the lip of the spout hangs down, it will drip every time you pour from it.

Apply the handle, dry, fire and glaze the same as the mug.

The sugar bowl

Form this the same way as the mug; but make the sides lower, *i.e.* 2½″. You can leave this without a handle or, if you prefer, put on two handles opposite each other.

Forming the spout of the cream jug.

The mug, cream jug and sugar bowl, partly dried.

MAKING YOUR OWN MOLDS

For some outside molded projects, you may not be able to find molds of the right size and shape; so you can make them. A useful form is the cylinder. Take a sheet of smooth, strong cardboard, and bend it into a cylinder of the required diameter. Wrap several bands of cellulose or gummed paper tape around the cylinder to hold it firm; also apply tape over the joint, so that the outside of the cylinder is smooth. Before applying clay, cover the cylinder with a sheet of newspaper, lightly stuck down with cellulose tape.

For big cylindrical molds, a good material is the lightweight steel sheet—either blued or tin-plated—that is used for making stove-pipes. You can buy it in sheets 2 feet square. Cut it to the required size with tin-snips, or old household scissors. Or score it heavily with a ruler and paring knife; turn it over and score heavily on the other side, in the same place; then bend it over the edge of a table and it will break. To hold this metal sheet in cylindrical form, stick it with insulating tape. Cover it with newspaper before applying the clay.

Similarly, cardboard or sheet metal can be made into any rectangular, triangular, or other shape of mold that you want.

A TABLE LAMP

Here's a good project to be formed on a home-made mold, I'm deliberately recommending a small lamp for a start; I suggest that you make this, and several more fairly small such projects, before you try a big one.

The main part of the lamp is a clay cylinder 5″ outside diameter, 6½″ high; the base is a smaller cylinder, 4″ outside diameter, 1″ high.

Making the molds.

Make two cardboard cylinders, one 4½″ diameter and 6½″ high, the other 3½″ diameter and 1″ high. Cover both with newspaper, held in place by cellulose tape.

The clay forms.

Roll out a slab of clay 16″ x 6½″ x ¼″ thick. Form it over the larger mold. Support the mold inside with one hand, use your thumb and, if necessary, a modeling tool, to weld the joint smooth.

Roll out another slab, 12¾″ x 1″ x ¼″ thick; similarly form it around the smaller mold.

Now roll out another slab about 6″ square and ¼″ thick. Take the larger clay cylinder, (still on the mold) and stand it on this slab. With a knife, cut around 1/16″ outside the cylinder. Lift the cylinder away and remove waste clay; you have a disk that is a little bigger than the end of your cylinder.

Put this disk on a paper-covered bat and place the cylinder on it, exactly centered. Now, with fingers supporting the lower end of the cylinder inside, weld the disk to the end of the cylinder. Work the clay up from the outer edge of the disk, welding it to the lower end of the cylinder all around. (This overlap helps to strengthen the joint.) Smooth the newly-formed joint with your fingers, then with a sponge. Leave the cylinder uncovered to firm up while you work on the next step.

Similarly cut another clay disk, ¼″ thick, 1/16″ bigger all around than the smaller cylinder; put it on a paper-covered bat; set the small cylinder on it, weld the joint firmly, and smooth it off.

Each of your two cylinders now has one end completely closed in by a disk of clay.

As soon as the clay has firmed up enough, slide the cylinders off the molds; to move the clay easily, slide the newspaper with it. If the joints of the cylinders are not smooth inside, use gentle finger pressure inside and out to complete the welding. If, by accident, you push either cylinder out of shape, simply slide it back on the mold again to correct the distortion, first applying a fresh newspaper lining; then slide it off once more.

Then cover the two cylinders with plastic and leave them to dry in the usual way till they are leather-hard.

Cutting.

When both cylinders are leather-hard, you can proceed with the cutting that gives the lamp its final shape.

Cut a circular hole, ½" diameter, in the center of the disk at the end of each cylinder. This will take the end of the lamp-socket. Then, with the blunt end of a pencil, make a hole in the side of the smaller cylinder to take the electric cord.

Now for the cut-out pattern. Make two cardboard templates, one to the leaf-shape, one to the diamond-shape shown.

Use the leaf-shape first. With two straight pins, fasten it to the larger cylinder, with its point ½" down from the top. with the narrow end of the bobby-pin tool (or some similar cutter) incise a line ⅛" wide and ⅛" deep around the template.

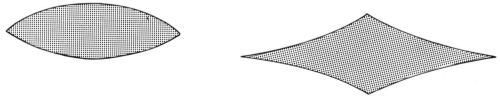

Leaf-shape and diamond-shape templates.

Now remove the template and cut around, just inside the incised line, with a sharp-pointed knife; support the clay inside with your hand until the section is cut cleanly out. Important: insert the blade at right-angles to the clay surface—not on the slant.

Now pin the template exactly below its first position, with its lower point ½″ up from the bottom of the cylinder. Repeat the incising and cutting.

Next, incise and cut another pair of holes exactly opposite to the first pair. With these pairs as a guide, cut four more pairs of holes, evenly spaced around the cylinder. (Total: 6 pairs.)

Then pin the diamond-shaped template in place, centered between two pairs of leaf-shaped holes; similarly incise and cut around it. Repeat until you have 6 diamond-shaped holes.

(Note: you can save the leaf-shaped and diamond-shaped cut-out pieces. Pierce a hole near the top of each; dry and fire them, glaze if you like, and use them as wind-chimes.)

Incising a line around the template.

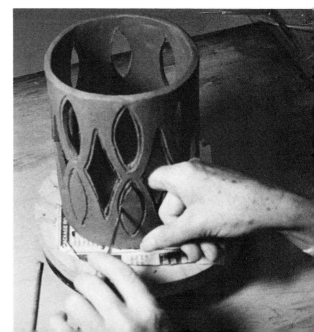

Cutting out the hole. The knife is kept close to the incised line, and the clay is supported inside with one finger, so that it will not be deformed by the pressure of the knife.

Firing and Finishing.

It's not essential to glaze this lamp. If you decide not to do so, fire to cone 04; this will make the cylinders stronger. Then color the outside with wood stain, antique it, or give it a gunmetal finish with stove polish. (For details, see Chapter 10.)

If you decide to glaze, fire first to cone 06; then apply the glaze—white, or the color of your choice and fire to cone 04. It's not necessary to glaze the inside, except perhaps 1″ down from the top. Anyway, don't glaze the disks that close off the cylinder-ends. After glazing you can, if you like, antique the outside of the large cylinder.

Assembly.

Glue the two sections together, using a household resin glue. Insert the lamp cord, connect it to the socket and screw the socket in place. Make a lining for the top cylinder from fiberglass fabric (it's fireproof). Measure, cut and staple the edges together to make a cylinder, and slip it inside the lamp. There's no need to glue it in place.

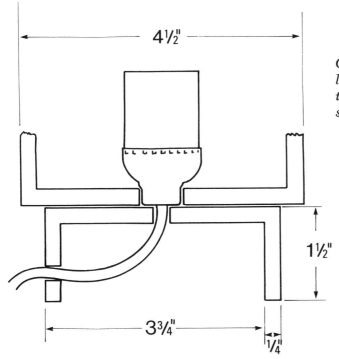

Cross-section of lower half of lamp, showing assembly of the two clay parts, lamp cord, and socket.

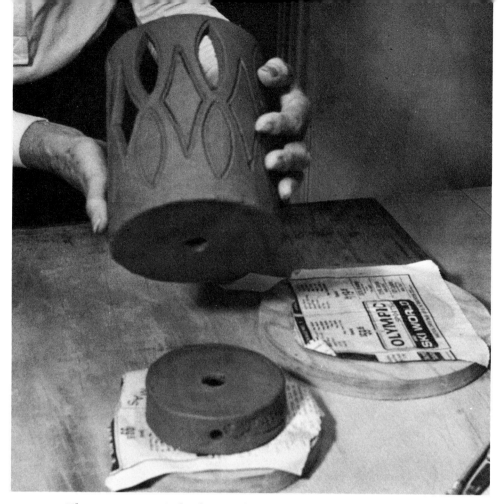

The two parts of the lamp, showing placement of the holes for the lamp socket and cord.

HANGING LAMPS

For a hanging lamp, make a cylinder with one end closed, exactly like the upper part of the table lamp described above; carve, fire, and finish in the same way. Insert the lamp socket and hang the lamp, open end down, by the electric cord; or, if you prefer, cover the cord with a chain. These lamps look particularly effective in groups of two or three, suspended at different heights.

CANDLE HOLDER

Make a cylinder like the upper part of the electric table lamp, 4″ across and 6″ high, and carve it in the same way, except that you don't need the ½″ hole in the center of the bottom disk.

As a mount for the candle, make a clay disk 3½″ across, ½″ thick. At its center cut a hole a little larger than the diameter of the candles you are going to use. This disk is not going to be fixed in place; you just stick the candle upright in the hole, then lower it to the bottom of the cylinder. This arrangement allows easy insertion and removal of candles, and prevents accumulation of wax drippings at the bottom of the cylinder. (As an alternative, you can buy a small glass candleholder to set the candle in and stand inside the cylinder.)

A lining of glass fiber for the cylinder is optional. With or without it, the candle holder makes a pretty centerpiece for the table.

A COVERED JAR

Here's a small jar, 4″ high, 3½″ outside diameter, with a lid.
The mold.
Make a cardboard tube 3″ in diameter and 4″ or more in height; cover it with newspaper.
The jar.
Make a slab of clay 11″ x 4″ x ¼″ thick. Form it over the mold into a cylinder. Make a clay disk 3½″ in diameter, ¼″ thick. Let both parts stand uncovered for about 20 minutes to firm up.

Roughen ¼″ in from the edge of the disk. Slide the cylinder off the mold and roughen its lower rim. Stick cylinder and disk together with slip; there's the body of your jar. Cover it to dry till leather-hard.
The lid.
Cut a disk 3¾″ in diameter, ¼″ thick. Make another disk 2⅞″ in diameter, but only ⅛″ thick. While they are still soft, stick them together; a coating

of slip and light finger pressure will make them adhere. (When the lid is finished and fired, this smaller disk keeps it from slipping off the jar.)

Make a knob and stick it to the lid, when both are leather-hard.

The jar, lid and knob at the leather-hard stage; see how the lid is formed so that it rests firmly on top of the jar.

Firing.

Fire first to cone 06 with the lid in place. Glaze to some color of your choice, taking special care not to get any glaze on the upper rim of the jar, or on the under-side of the lid where it touches the rim; if you do, they will stick together on the glaze firing.

THE CYLINDER FORM

Here are some hints for using the cylinder form in original projects.

1. Bear in mind that you do not have to mold your clay the full height of the cylinder. From the same cylinder mold you can make several different clay forms, of different heights.

2. For planning the thickness of the clay sheet. you can follow this general rule:

Less than 7″ high: ¼″ thick.
More than 7″ high: ⅜″ thick.

3. For cutting the clay sheet, measure circumference of the cylindrical mold with a tape measure and add ¼″ or thereabouts for overlap and welding.

CREATIVE MOLD FORMING

Remember that the shape you produce by inside or outside mold forming need not always be accepted as a finished pot; there is much that you can do to modify it. To make a shallow pot deeper, you can heighten the sides by strip forming above the level of whatever piece you are using for a mold; this would be done while the clay is soft.

Or, at the leather-hard stage, you can stick a base, handles or knobs, or carve an incised pattern, on a piece that had a smooth, featureless exterior as it came from the mold.

In other words, you can make your pot *better, more interesting*, than the mold from which you shaped it!

10

Finishing

In this chapter I shall describe a number of processes that can be used on pots before and after they are fired, to make them more useful or more beautiful.

POLISHING

For a rich, black finish on pots that have been biscuit-fired, apply black shoe-polish and keep rubbing it in until no more comes off on the cloth; then the black finish is permanent. Black stove-polish is even better: well rubbed in, it gives a beautiful gunmetal effect.

STAINING

Here's a process that is particularly good on pieces that have been burnished and biscuit fired. Get some wood-stain. Mahogany and walnut are good, but other colors such as green, blue, or gold may also be used. Apply the stain thinly with a cloth; it soaks in quickly. Add more for a more intense color. Always rub the color in well, to be sure it does not come off later. For a glossy effect, you can finish by rubbing in a clear wax.

WATERPROOFING

Glazing is the traditional method of waterproofing a pot; but there is another technique you can use for some pots if you want to avoid the trouble of a second firing. Melt some paraffin wax, pour it into the pot, swish it around inside so that it covers all the sides, and pour it out quickly. This is good for a narrow-necked vase; it would not look well in a bowl, and of course would not be suitable for foods or beverages.

ENGOBE DESIGN

At the leather-hard stage you can paint a design on the pot in engobe of one, two, or more colors. Complete the drying, and fire as usual. See the item "Engobe" in Chapter 3 for hints on varying color intensity and heightening color values.

WAX-RESIST

Here is a different method of using engobe. Buy some wax-resist from the ceramic supply store. It is a thick, glue-like liquid in a jar. (If it is too thick to work with, thin it with a little water.)

Paint your design on the pot with a brush, using this wax-resist liquid, when the pot is leather-hard. The wax-resist quickly sets to a hard layer. Now apply one or more coats of engobe all over the pot, covering the wax and all.

Complete the drying, and fire the pot as usual, to cone 06. As it gets hot, the wax melts and prevents the engobe from adhering, so where the wax had been, you see the natural color of the pot.

It's nice to put a transparent glaze over such a design, with a second firing to cone 04.

SGRAFFITO

The name of this technique is derived from an Italian word meaning "scratched." At the leather-hard stage you paint the pot all over with engobe. Then, with a pencil, a knitting needle, or a pointed stick, you scratch a thin design into the engobe, so as to expose the clay beneath. When fired, this design shows in the natural color of the clay. Here again, many potters like to apply a transparent glaze over such a design.

ANTIQUING

This process is good for a piece that has been carved, or that has a raised design; you do the antiquing after the pot is completely finished, biscuit fired, and glazed. You can also apply the process to biscuit-fired, unglazed pieces.

The materials are metallic pastes, obtainable in tubes (like toothpaste) from craft stores and some hardware stores. Copper, gold and silver are the most useful colors.

Copper

For the best effect, use *very little* of the paste. Squeeze out at most ¼" on to a smooth metal surface such as a jar-lid. Touch one finger to the paste; then rub the finger briskly on the bare metal to get the paste evenly distributed over the finger-tip.

Now rub the finger lightly over the pot, so that the copper just highlights the raised part of the design. If you don't get quite enough color the first time, take a little more on your finger and rub again. But don't be over-eager: it's best to start with too little. If you put on too much, you get a solid metallic covering instead of the desired antique effect.

This antiquing is a rather delicate operation; so before you try it on a good pot, practice on a few small pieces of biscuit-ware to get used to the technique.

Copper and Gold

For a still better effect, put on copper first, as described above, then by the same method, apply gold paste over the copper—always applying it very lightly.

Silver

Silver paste also gives a good antique effect—by itself on a dark-colored clay, or over gold. Silver is particularly effective on a matt glaze—less so on a shiny glaze.

Silver can also be used effectively on a box or lamp that has been carved and biscuit fired, but not glazed.

Caution

I would stress that antiqued pieces are not suitable for heavy use, such as putting through a dishwasher. It's a process suitable mainly for decorative effect. (Antiqued pieces can, if necessary, be carefully washed by hand when dirty.)

METAL FINISH

You can give a complete covering of metal paste to biscuit-fired, unglazed ware; apply it with your finger, as for antiquing, but cover the entire surface, rubbing it in well. Note that this produces an entirely different effect from antiquing.

LATEX PAINTS

Exterior latex paint is excellent for coloring biscuit-fired ware that is not to be glazed. It is available in a wide range of colors, in small cans; it goes on easily, dries quickly, and the brushes wash clean with water. I mentioned that this paint dries quickly; that is, it soon reaches a condition where it won't rub off on your hands. But after application, it goes through a gradual hardening process that takes several days. When the hardening is complete, you have a very tough surface that will stand up to a good deal of wear and tear (though not scouring or putting through a dishwasher!).

UNDERGLAZE COLORS

Here is another way of painting a colored design on pottery. You can mix the ingredients yourself, making only as much as you want to use each time. There's no need for precise measurement—just stir a tiny pinch of the chemical into one or two teaspoons of water.

For green: copper oxide
For blue: cobalt oxide
For red: iron oxide
For black: manganese dioxide

Apply with a watercolor brush to fully-dried greenware, then give the usual first firing. As the name of this method suggests, these colors, for best effect, should be covered with a clear glaze on second firing.

If you have some left over, it can be stored in a little glass jar for future use.

I have listed only a few of the most useful colors here. A ceramic supply store can show you many more.

LINING

By putting in a lining of velvet, you can turn a ceramic cigaret box into a nice looking jewel box. Stick the velvet in place with white household glue.

FELT PADS

Lamps, cigaret boxes, jewel boxes—any such pieces may scratch your furniture unless you take the precaution of adding protective pads. Cut small pieces of felt, and fasten them to the corners of the base with glue.

Coil-formed table lamp. The finger-marks were deliberately left on the lamp, to give it an interesting texture. The lamp was covered with a white glaze, and mounted on a black wooden base.

FINISHING METHODS FOR CHILDREN

It's best not to let small children use glazes, underglaze colors or engobes. Instead, they can color biscuit-fired pieces with wax crayons, watercolors, latex paints, or poster paints. A simple substitute for glazing to heighten colors and give a shiny surface, is to cover the pot with clear, no-buff floor polish. There's scope for experiment here: some types of polish give a sparkling effect. Two coats of the polish will give a more brilliant gloss than one.

11

Glazing

A GLAZE is a thin layer of glass welded, by firing, to part or all of the surface of a pot. The glaze may be clear (i.e. the clay shows through it) or opaque (i.e. it completely covers the clay); it may be colored or colorless; it may be smooth, matt, or textured. The glaze serves one, or both, of two purposes—to make the pot waterproof, or to improve its appearance.

The usual procedure is first to give a piece of greenware the biscuit firing that produces the irreversible change from clay into pottery. Glaze is applied on a second firing, at a higher temperature, that melts the glaze ingredients and fuses them firmly to the body of the pot.

You can't glaze a pot on the biscuit firing because at this stage the combined water is being driven off from the clay in the form of steam; the only way it can escape is through the pores of the clay. But if all these pores were sealed with glaze, then the pot would explode!

Another reason: on many projects, you will get best results by firing the glaze at a somewhat higher temperature than was used for the biscuit firing—cone 06 for biscuit, and cone 04 for glaze.

So, for pieces that are to be glazed—mugs, soup bowls, plates,—we follow the two-firings procedure.

CHOICE OF GLAZES

Here are some principles that should be followed in buying or making glazes.

The glaze must suit the body of the pot.

1. In its rate of expansion. If, during the firing and subsequent cooling, the glaze and the pot are expanding and contracting at different rates, the glaze will be cracked or shattered.

2. In the temperature required to vitrify it. It's no use choosing a beautiful glaze that requires a very high temperature if, before you attain that temperature, the body of the pot has melted! For most projects in this book, I've recommended glazes that vitrify at cone 04; at that temperature the glaze, and the clay we are using, will adhere perfectly.

The glaze must suit the purpose for which the pot is to be used. For tableware, the glaze should be smooth; a rough glaze would impede dishwashing; and, even though the pots were in fact clean, they would always look somewhat dull and dirty.

For all pots that are to contain food and beverages, it's essential to use lead-free glazes. Lead glazes are excellent for some other purposes but, if used on tableware, carry the risk of giving you lead poisoning (a dangerous condition with severe stomach pain, cramps in arms and legs, anemia and, in some cases, lasting damage to the nervous system).

The glaze must suit the size and form of the piece. A brilliantly reflective glaze might look well on a necklace or pair of earrings; but the same glaze could be out of place on a deeply-incised flower bowl, because you don't want the bowl to sparkle like a huge jewel when a light shines on it!

BUYING GLAZES

I suggest that you work at first with ready-mixed glazes. You have enough on your hands, learning to make well-designed, strong, good-looking pots. After you have acquired a certain amount of skill in that department there will be plenty of time to proceed to making your own glazes.

All ceramic supply stores sell ready-mixed glazes, both in powder and liquid form. I would recommend that you begin with the liquid ones.

Tell the storekeeper what clay you have used for the body of the pot, what firing temperature you intend to use for the glazing (in most of these projects, cone 04), and what color you want to achieve; he will advise you what glazes will be suitable.

Remember that glaze is not like paint! The color of the glaze as you buy it is no guide to the final color of the pot on which you use it: that is developed only by firing. You may have three glazes that all look white; but after firing, one turns red, one green, and one black.

If you decide to buy the powdered glaze, you will need an 80-mesh sieve to use when mixing it. First mix the powder with enough water to give a thick, creamy consistency. (Two fluid ounces of water for each 3 ounces weight of dry ingredients is usually about right.) Then pour the paste on to the sieve, and work it through the mesh with a 1″ paint brush, to strain out lumps. You can store glazes indefinitely in screw-capped jars.

APPLYING GLAZE

Pots that are ready for glazing have already been fired once, and may have been standing around for days or weeks, gathering dust, fragments of clay, etc. That dirt can spoil the effect of your glaze; so before you start glazing wipe each pot with a damp sponge.

The glaze, too, whether you bought it in liquid form, or mixed it yourself, may have been standing around for some time; so, before you use it, check its consistency. Stir it well with a stick. If you find it lumpy, put it through your 80-mesh sieve. Then try a brush-load on a pot, and note how it feels—too thick, too thin, or just right. You'll know it's just right if, when you apply it, it goes on easily and smoothly, like well-mixed, thin paint.

If it's not right, proceed as follows:
Glaze too thick.
Dilute it with a little water, and stir thoroughly.

Glaze too thin.

If the glaze is too thin and runny, let it stand for 2 or 3 hours; some water will come to the top, and you can carefully pour it off. Then stir and test again.

The label on the jar usually says how many coats of glaze are required; three coats is about average. Apply the first coat and let it dry; this usually takes only a few minutes, because the biscuit-fired pot is porous. Similarly apply the second coat and let it dry; then apply the third coat. It's best to let the pot dry overnight before firing it.

For a tile that is to be glazed on one side only, simply paint the glaze on the face side.

For a bowl or vase that is to be glazed on both sides, a convenient way is to pour the glaze into the inside, tilt the vase so that all the inner surface is covered, then pour the glaze out. Next paint the outside. Repeat for each coat of glaze.

Unglazed Areas

It's best not to put glaze on the base of a pot, or on firing it will stick to the floor or shelf of the kiln. (You can see the unglazed base area on many commercially-made mugs, vases, teapots, etc.) If the pot has a recessed bottom, like the jug in photo on p. 76, then you can glaze the recess (that won't touch the kiln) and leave bare only the rim around the outside.

This process of leaving the base unglazed is called "dry-footing."

If, by accident, you get glaze on an area you wanted to leave bare, wait till it is dry, and sandpaper the glaze off, or scrape it off with a knife, then wipe with a damp sponge.

Also, if you are glazing a piece with a lid, put no glaze on the area where the lid touches the body of the pot, or they will stick together in firing. A useful method here is, before you apply the glaze, to put wax-resist on the rim of the pot, and on the corresponding area of the lid. Give it a few minutes to dry; then you can apply the glaze without worrying about sticking.

Two-Color Effects

You can apply two different-colored glazes at one firing if you wish. Here for example, is how I made a two-colored dish. The main glaze was a glossy orange. I applied three coats of that, and let them dry. Then I took a little of the same glaze, and put in a pinch of manganese and a pinch of cobalt. I applied a thick coating of this around the rim of the dish. On firing, it turned a rich black, which ran down the sides of the dish.

You can try for similar effects with various dark colors. For brown, add a pinch of manganese and three pinches of red iron oxide. For deep green, add a pinch of copper oxide (exact measurement isn't necessary here.)

It's important, for best results, to get plenty of the dark glaze on the rim. If you can't get a really thick layer in one coat, let it dry and apply a second coat.

This method is not suitable for use with matt glazes; they don't run as do the glossy ones.

REGLAZING

In Chapter 6, I described the method of glaze firing. There should not be any serious technical problems with it. Yet glaze firing is not an exact science: it's always something of an excitement, a surprise. Even though you use the same glaze on the same type of clay, you cannot guarantee precisely the same results every time. One reason is that there's always some slight variation in timing—even a few seconds' difference may change the nature of the finished glaze.

Suppose you find, after firing, that a pot has not got enough glaze, or the glaze has not produced quite the effect you want. The pot is not spoiled! You can easily give it a reglaze.

Warm the pot in the kitchen oven to 66°C. (150°F.) before you begin. That was not necessary when you first applied glaze to the porous, biscuit-fired surface; but the new glaze might not adhere well to a cold glazed surface. So warm the pot; put on your first coat of glaze and let it dry. For the second and third coats, similarly warm the pot each time.

As for choice of glaze on reglazing, you have several options: you can use exactly the same glaze again; or you can use glaze of the same formula at a lighter or darker color.

Fire to the same temperature as on the first glaze firing. The two colors may melt and blend, and give you some unexpected, pleasing effects.

If you are still not satisfied with the results, there's no reason why you shouldn't try still another reglaze.

CAUTION

Many ingredients of glazes are poisonous. Do not let children play with glazes. Don't let them handle, or suck, unfired pots that have glaze on them. Don't let glaze material get into cuts on your hands (wear rubber gloves if necessary). When mixing dry powdered ingredients, wrap a piece of cloth over your nose and mouth to avoid inhaling the dust. After working with glaze, whether wet or dry, wash your hands before you handle food or beverages.

I don't want to scare you away from using glazes; I've handled them for years without mishap, and so have thousands of other potters. Just use the same degree of care as you do with everyday hazards such as disinfectants and boiling water!

MIXING YOUR OWN GLAZES

Most of the published glaze recipes require considerably higher temperatures than the cone 04 that we are using. If you take recipes from other sources, be sure to check their firing temperatures before you go to the trouble of getting ingredients.

I will first give the recipes, then offer some hints for mixing them.

Two Leadless Glazes

The following recipes produce glazes that are safe for use on tableware. (Remember that glazes containing lead should not be used in contact with foods or beverages.)

White Glaze

This glaze can be fired from cone 07 to cone 04; best results will be obtained at cone 04.

Leadless frit	100 grams
Ball clay	10 grams
Tin oxide	10 grams

or instead of the tin oxide use

Zircopax	20 grams

This recipe gives a whitish glaze, but by using suitable additives you can get a good range of colors.

For turquoise add 1 gram copper oxide

For blue add ½ gram cobalt oxide

This is a translucent glaze; underglaze colors will show through it.

For yellow add 2 grams yellow underglaze color

For green add 1 gram chromium oxide

For purple add 1 gram manganese dioxide

For brown add 2 grams red iron oxide

For other colors, you can experiment with underglaze colors in similar proportions.

Cloudy Blue Glaze

This glaze can be fired from cone 06 to cone 04.

Colemanite	65.5 grams
Kaolin (china clay)	9.3 grams
Flint	25.2 grams
Cobalt carbonate	1 gram

For other colors, omit the cobalt carbonate, and add the same coloring ingredients that were listed under the previous glaze recipe.

This is a translucent glaze; underglaze colors will show through it.

Three Glazes Containing Lead
Rutile Satin Matt Glaze

This should be fired at cone 04. The basic formula gives a lovely ivory, translucent, so that underglaze colors will show through it,

White lead	150.5 grams
Feldspar	42.5 grams
Kaolin	3.75 grams
Flint	43.4 grams
Rutile	11.4 grams
Whiting	3.75 grams
Borax	28.75 grams
Calcined kaolin	6.75 grams
Tin	10.00 grams

(To make calcined kaolin, take some ordinary kaolin, put it in a pot that has previously been bisque-fired, but not glazed, and put it in your kiln some time when you are firing to cone 06. Make a fair-sized batch, weigh out what you need for this recipe, and store the rest for future use.)

For a greeny-brown flecked coloration, add to the basic recipe:

Copper oxide	3 grams
Manganese	1 gram

For blue, add to the basic formula:

Copper oxide	1 gram
Cobalt	1 gram

For turquoise, add to the basic formula:

Copper oxide	4½ grams
Cobalt oxide	1 gram

Barium Matt Glaze

This glaze should be fired to cone 04. *Do not* use the basic formula alone; but add either the Turquoise #1 or the Turquoise #2 colorants, to get a lovely glaze that is specially good for decorative pieces and sculptures.

White lead	167.7 grams
Whiting	18.8 grams
Feldspar	42.3 grams
Kaolin	43.8 grams
Flint	30.0 grams
Barium carbonate	15.6 grams

For Turquoise #1 add to the basic formula:

Copper oxide	4.5 grams
Cobalt oxide	0.75 grams

For Turquoise #2 add to the basic formula:

Copper carbonate	4.0 grams
Cobalt oxide	0.06 grams

This glaze is opaque, and will not let underglaze colors show through it.

Transparent Lead Glaze.

This glaze can be fired from cone 06 to cone 02.

White lead	142.0 grams
Whiting	35.0 grams
Feldspare	60.0 grams
Kaolin	22.0 grams
Flint	47.0 grams

The basic formula gives a clear, colorless glaze. You can, if you wish, give it a color, while still maintaining the transparency.

For blue, add to the basic formula:

Cobalt oxide	2.0 grams

For green, add to the basic formula:

Copper oxide	3.0 grams

Sculpture by Arthur Freeman.

Three shallow mold-formed bowls.

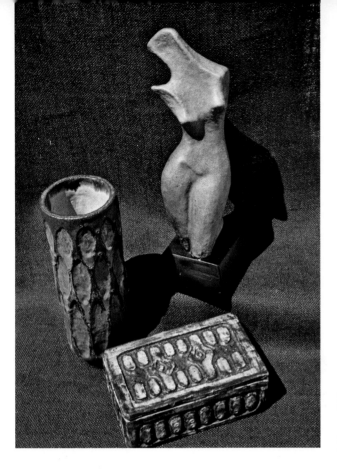

Cigaret box, sculpture and vase.

Head of Chinese man.

Covered jar, bowl and two ashtrays.

Two vases and jewel box.

Vase and plate.

Tile table by Gisela Kaempffer: incised design, satin matt glaze.

Bottle and two covered candy jars.

Potentate, wife and concubine.

Vase.

Matching candy jar and cigaret box.

Sculpture

Additives

There are two additives that should be used in any home-mixed glaze. They have no effect on color or texture of the glaze after firing, but they are very useful in the mixing and application.

1. To each batch of glaze, add 1 teaspoon of Epsom salts (magnesium sulphate). A little more or less does not matter. It helps to keep the glaze mixture homogeneous during the time you are applying it. Without this, the heavier ingredients tend to settle to the bottom.

2. Get an ounce of gum tragacanth from the drugstore. (It's a whitish powder produced from a shrub that grows in Asia Minor.) Mix 1 level teaspoon of the gum with 1 fluid ounce of alcohol (methyl hydrate) then add 1 pint of water. (If the powdered gum seems lumpy, put it through your sieve before dissolving it.) Keep the solution on hand for use when mixing glazes. Add about 1 tablespoon of it to each batch of glaze you mix. It makes the glaze flow on more easily and uniformly, and also helps it stick to the pot when it dries, before firing. You can get gum tragacanth solution, mixed and ready to use, from the ceramic supply store.

Mixing

Put the measured recipe ingredients in a bowl. Add water, a little at a time, stirring with a 1″ brush, until the mixture has a thick, creamy consistency. Push the mixture through the 80-mesh sieve. Then add the teaspoon of Epsom salts and the tablespoon of gum solution.

Size of Batches

A batch of ingredients weighing roughly 300 grams is a good size; it mixes up to about a pint of glaze. But when you are trying a recipe for the first time, I would suggest making up about 100 grams dry ingredients, to see if you like the glaze after you have applied it to your pots and fired it. In appreciation of glazes, as in so many aspects of the potter's art, much depends on personal taste; a glaze that, in color and texture, delights me may not please you at all.

12

Design for Pottery

AFTER you have made a number of the pots described elsewhere in this book, you will no doubt want to go ahead and design pots to your own requirements. In this chapter, then, I offer some thoughts that will help you in creating such designs.

HAND-MADE FORMS

I would stress, first of all, that we are thinking of, and designing, *hand-made* pottery. It is not supposed to look perfectly regular, perfectly smooth; you are not trying to turn out half-dozen sets of absolutely identical cups, dishes, or vases. Machines can do that. You want to do something that a machine can't do—give some touch of your own creativity, your own taste, to each piece you produce.

DESIGN AND FUNCTION

A major test for good design is to see how the finished piece fulfills its function: "How well does it do what it's supposed to do?"

Consider, for example, a cup. Is it a convenient size to drink from? Is the handle convenient for the fingers to grasp?

Or take a jug. Does it stand firm and stable when full of water, lemonade, or whatever it's meant to hold? Is the spout properly shaped, so that it pours cleanly without dribbling?

Consider a planter. Is it the right depth, length and breadth for the kind of plant it is supposed to accommodate?

A flower-vase: does it hold water properly? Or does it leak over the shelf or table it stands on?

A trivet: does it stand firm itself, and will the teapot or coffee pot stand stable and level on it?

Or how do we judge the design of a lamp? Is it convenient for fitting the wiring, lamp socket and, if necessary, the switch? Is it stable and heavy enough so that it won't easily be knocked over? Does it emit a satisfactory amount of light in a pattern that is useful for reading, eating, or whatever particular lighting function it is supposed to fill?

If the piece does not fulfill its function, then no matter how much clay, glaze, thought and labor went into making it, it is a failure.

APPEARANCE

In addition to fulfilling its proper function, a well-designed piece of pottery looks good in the environment where it is being used. I can't lay down arbitrary rules as to what looks good where. A pot that perfectly suits a country cottage might look out of place in a large city home, or in a high-rise apartment.

A well-designed lamp not only emits adequate light; it should *look good* in its own light, and also in the light of other lamps, and daylight.

A well-designed planter not only stands stable when full of earth: its appearance harmonizes with the plants that are to grow in it.

A piece of tableware, in color, texture and pattern, should go well with the kind of food or drink which it is to contain. Many people, for example, would find it unpleasant to eat food off a black or red plate, or to drink beer from an orange mug.

SHAPE

I think it's worth emphasizing that there's nothing specially significant about *round* shapes. We see so many round pots—cups, mugs, plates, casseroles, planters, and so on—that some people get the idea that *all* pots have to be round!

This emphasis on roundness, in fact, is just part of the influence of the wheel. (Obviously, round forms are easy and effective to produce on the wheel.) But here we are working without the wheel, so we have full freedom to make pots three-sided, four-sided, five-sided, oval, or any shape we like.

Two bowls. The smaller one is oblong, 8" x 5" at the top, with the corners rounded, and 2" deep. The larger bowl was inside-molded in a shallow bowl with clay ⅜" thick. To deepen it, another strip 1½" wide was added around the rim. Careful inspection will show the joint. A 1" strip was used to make the circular base. Finish: blue glaze with gold antiquing.

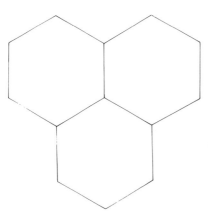

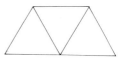

Some combinations of non-square tile shapes.

The plate was molded inside another plate, and the incised design created at the leather-hard stage. The vase is coil-formed, with an incised design.

In your pottery design, then, try to be unconventional, adventurous. Tiles, for example, don't all have to be square or oblong. Three-sided or six-sided tiles can be fitted together to cover a table-top or make a wall-plaque; so can a combination of squares and octagons drawn on the same length side.

While I'm on this question of shape, I should perhaps repeat what I've suggested elsewhere, that there's no particular merit in *symmetry* for its own sake. A good design may be symmetrical. But a design can be non-symmetrical, and yet be excellent.

There's a point about shape mentioned in Chapter 4, which is worth re-emphasizing. Glaze will not hold on sharp edges and corners, so these formations should be avoided in ceramic design. If you can't help making sharp edges and corners at an early stage of shaping a pot (as in cutting slabs or blocks of clay with a knife) then they must, before the pot is fired, be rounded off a little with a sponge, or with your thumb. Glass, metal, wood, and plastics can effectively be given sharp edges and corners, but not pottery. The shapes you create must be in accord with the inherent qualities of the material you are using.

PROPORTION

As a general rule, the thickness of the material should be proportional to the size of the piece. Your decisions on thickness must also take into account such factors as incised decoration; if you plan deep incising, then the walls of the vase or bowl must be made thicker to allow for it. The strength of the pot is that of its thinnest spot!

The size of a pattern—whether in relief, in engobe, or any other medium—should be proportional to the total size of the piece.

Consider also the proportion of the piece that is covered by a pattern to that which is left plain. For example, you can have a design—symmetrical or a doodle—repeated all around a vase; or you can have a simple design going just up one side of the vase, and all the rest left undecorated. Similarly with a plate or bowl: you can use an all-over design, or just a single design element, placed in the center, or to one side.

STUDYING GOOD DESIGNS

Here are some ideas for forming an appreciation of good design in pottery; the same methods will develop your ability to create good designs yourself.

1. Whenever you see pottery—in stores, museums, other people's homes —don't just let yourself think, "I like this piece" or "I don't like that piece."

Make yourself analyze each piece, till you can tell *exactly what it is that you like or dislike* about it! You may sometimes find that a piece has several good points, but one bad flaw; you may see another piece that is generally bad, yet does have one good feature. In each case, by separating good from bad, you are sharpening your own taste.

In other words, you seek in each piece of pottery features that are worthy of imitation; you also seek features that should be avoided.

There is nothing dishonorable about this: it's the way that workers in all media have learned their craft all down the ages.

2. Besides studying the esthetic effect of the pots you see, study also the technical means used to produce them. Ask questions if necessary. To

be sure, you may run up against some potters who are secretive; but you'll find many who enjoy telling how they do their work.

3. Build a photo-collection of what you consider to be well-designed and well-made pieces. Clip photos from magazines, newspapers, catalogues. Analyze their good and bad points as suggested above. Review the file from time to time, to impress the ideas on your mind. Look into it when you are seeking inspiration for some original work.

CREATING ORIGINAL DESIGNS

I suggest that you gain experience by following the designs in this book and, where necessary, using templates to check the progress of your work. Then, after a while, you find you are developing your manual skill and your understanding of clay as a medium; you find that, while you are working on a pot, you already have a fair idea of how it is going to turn out.

That's the time to begin creating directly with the clay, making pots to express your own personal requirements and tastes.

You have one important advantage. This is not like carving marble! If a pot doesn't turn out to your satisfaction, you can just squash it and start again. Every potter has done this, and has had the pleasure of learning something by so doing.

PERSONAL TASTE

I would like to emphasize the importance of working to gratify your own taste. I have described in this book pieces that please me. I know that they please quite a number of other people, too. If you want to make pots to sell, then you must cater to the taste of your customers; but if you are making a pot for yourself, you must be the judge of its merit. No matter what other people may say against a piece of your pottery, if it suits your needs, and if you are happy to live with it, then for you it is good!

13

Other Methods

HERE are some additional techniques and pieces of equipment that you may like to make or use after you have mastered the contents of the preceding chapters.

HARD-SLAB FORMING

In Chapter 4, I described several methods for shaping a slab of clay while it is still soft and flexible. Here is a somewhat more difficult technique that uses clay slabs that are dried enough to hold shape in handling, but are not yet leather-hard. It's well suited to the making of rectangular forms—cigaret boxes, candy boxes, jewel boxes and so on.

1. Begin by drawing an accurate, full-size set of plans for the box you want. Here are the plans for a jewel box.

Make cardboard templates for the various parts.

2. With rolling pin and wooden slats, make a slab ¼ inch thick and cut out the base, sides and lid. Roll out a ⅛″ slab for the inside piece of the lid.

It's important, in this method, to be accurate in the cutting of the pieces—all dimensions exact, all sides straight, all corners square, and so on. In some techniques I've described earlier, soft clay can be compressed or stretched to fit; but that won't work here.

The completed jewel box.

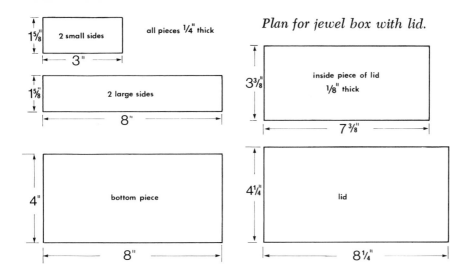

1⅝″ | 2 small sides | all pieces ¼″ thick

← 3″ →

Plan for jewel box with lid.

1⅝″ | 2 large sides

← 8″ →

3⅜″ | inside piece of lid
1⁄8″ thick

← 7⅜″ →

4″ | bottom piece

← 8″ →

4¼″ | lid

← 8¼″ →

3. Cover the pieces with plastic and start drying them. To avoid warping, follow the same procedure that I described in chapter 4 for tiles: turn all the pieces over twice daily until they are firm enough for handling.

4. Now, to assemble the parts, take a comb or hacksaw blade and roughen the clay at every point where two parts are to join. With finger or brush, apply a coating of slip and press the parts together. After a few seconds they will adhere. Roll out a coil of soft clay, ⅛ inch in diameter; work it thoroughly into the joints around the inside of the bottom and up the sides at the corners. Carve the pattern on the lid; stick on the inside piece. Put the lid on the box, cover the whole loosely with plastic, and leave it till fully dried.

5. Fire to cone 06.

6. You have several options for finishing the box. You can stain or polish it any color of your choice. Line it with velvet cut to size, and stuck in place with white resin glue. Stick a felt pad, ¾″ square, on each corner of the base, so that the clay won't scratch a dressing-table. (Or, if you prefer to leave it unlined, it will make a useful cigaret box.)

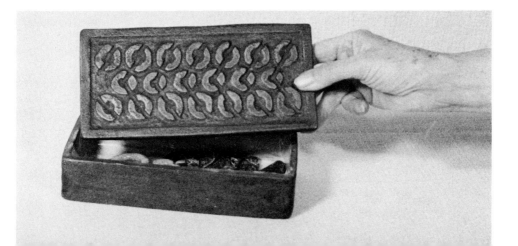

Rectangular lamp by Constance Wyndham.

Here are the dimensions for a lamp to be made by this same hard-slab forming method: 15″ high x 6″ x 4½″; the clay slab is ⅜″ thick.

You can, if you like, add a rectangular base to this lamp: make it 2″ high x 7″ x 5½″.

You can go on to design lamps, boxes, etc. in other shapes—triangular, hexagonal and so on. The only significant difference is that, for such shapes, you will have to miter the corners to make them fit.

Triangular and hexagonal cross-sections, showing mitering corners.

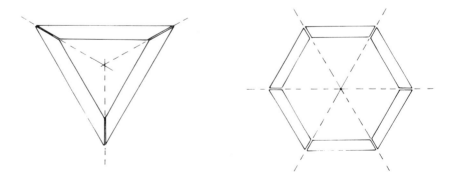

SCULPTURE

Sculpture is one of the most fascinating branches of ceramic work. But it's not easy! So it's best not to begin by promising to make a set of realistic portrait heads of your family and friends. It takes practice to achieve a good likeness. But you can very well begin with abstract or semi-abstract heads and then, if you wish, go on to representational ones.

Let's begin with a head about ¾ life size.

The Armature

The first step is to build an armature. This has two purposes. It supports the clay as you work on it. Secondly, it lets you make the head a not-too-thick shell of clay. There are severe technical problems in firing any solid piece in which the clay is more than 2″ thick; but the armature is removed before the head is fired, so the heat does not have to fire a solid head.

Get a hollow cardboard tube about 9″ long. (The tubes from rolls of paper towels or aluminum foil are good.) Make a ball of crumpled newspaper about 4″ across, compress it tightly around the top of the tube, and stick it in place with cellulose tape.

Note that the reason for having the armature thin in the neck is so that the clay will be thick enough to support the weight of the head.

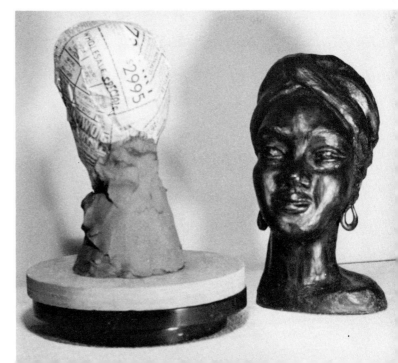

LEFT: *the armature for a ¾-size head. It is 8¾″ high. Part of the first layer of clay is in place; the lumps will be smoothed out as the work progresses.* RIGHT: *a head made by this method, biscuit fired, then colored with stove polish. Height, 9½″.*

Shaping The Head

When the armature is complete, stand it in the middle of a bat, and fix it in place by a one-inch collar of clay all around where the neck meets wood.

Now you can begin building the head. Starting at the bottom, cover the armature with clay; apply it in walnut-sized lumps; weld them together, and flatten them somewhat, as you go, working with your thumb. (For convenience, you may like to stand the bat and armature on a turntable, if you have one.) Proceed like this till the whole armature is covered, right to the top, with a uniform layer of clay, about ½ inch to 1 inch thick.

Now you can begin shaping the head, adding extra clay wherever it is needed—for nose, lips, ears, hair, etc.—and building it out to the size you want.

For shaping fine details—lips, ears, eyes, etc.—use whatever tool seems handiest—a knitting needle, a knife-point, a modeling tool, etc.

For a non-realistic effect, you can leave the face rough, with the texture of the original lumps of clay more or less visible. For a realistic skin texture, smooth the surface with your thumb.

For curly hair, take small pieces of clay, about thumbnail size, and slide them on. For straight, or softly waved hair, simply draw a comb over the soft clay.

It's a slow job; your first head won't be finished in one session or in two. (The first head I made, I worked on all of one summer in my spare time!) Between sessions, cover the head with a damp piece of heavy towel, and a plastic bag over that; this keeps the clay soft and workable till you have finished it.

Removing The Armature

You now have to take the armature out. If it were left in, the clay would shrink around it during further drying, and crack. To get at the armature, you are going to cut off the top of the head, just above the ears and eyebrows. Decide on the line where your cut will go, then make a light vertical scratch at the back of the head, crossing this line. (The scratch will ensure exact replacement of the top piece later.)

Take your cutting wire and cut off the top of the head; lift off the top and set it down gently.

The head is now fairly firm and, if you proceed with reasonable care, you won't deform it. So start to pull the armature out from the top, cutting the paper and cardboard where necessary to make it come out easily.

When all the armature is out; scratch with a comb around the two cut edges, moisten them with slip, and replace the top, matching up the two parts of the vertical scratch.

Cover up the main cut and the scratch by smoothing with your thumb, or using the appropriate tool to restore the effect of the hair.

Complete drying as usual, and fire to cone 06. You can finish the biscuit-fired head by polishing, staining, metal finish, latex paint, or some other method of your choice.

Figurines

Full-length figures can be made in the same general way. Here are some technical hints.

If the figure is going to be more than about 2″ thick, you will need an armature. I use the same kind of cardboard tube as for heads, but don't pad it out with paper. The top of the armature comes at the shoulder-line; there is no need for an armature inside the head, because it is small.

Mother, father and child group by Arthur Freeman. The clay is thin enough to need no armature. Note the simple abstract forms: no faces are needed. Man, 10¾″ high; woman, 9¼″ high; child, 5¾″ high; The wooden base is made from a 7″ equilateral triangle with the corners rounded off.

To show the feet and legs creates a problem of making the figurine stand up; I sometimes avoid that difficulty by making robed figures, which have a broad base. When the figure is finished, the armature is extracted through the bottom.

Carved Sculpture

So far I've discussed methods of making a sculpture by adding clay—building it from the center outwards; but you can, if you prefer, begin with a big lump of clay and produce your finished shape by cutting away. (Some purists will say that this method is appropriate for stone and wood, but not for clay; yet I see not the slightest objection to using it, if it suits your taste.)

I would suggest beginning with some fairly small projects. Pound a piece of well-wedged clay into a shape somewhat bigger than the form you want to make; then, with knife, modeling tool or wire loop, begin cutting away.

Work from the top downward; if you cut too much from the bottom at first, it won't support the weight of the top. You will also have to carefully gauge the rate at which you let the clay dry, so that it stays soft enough to work, yet not so soft as to collapse. Experimentation and gradual progression from small to larger works will guide you.

One important point is that, as you go on to larger carved works, you must design them so as not to have any part of the finished form too thick. If you positively require a section over 2″ thick, you had better cut it in half with your wire, scoop out part of the clay from inside, and rejoin it.

Note that in any such hollowed-out piece, you should pierce several holes, with a fairly thick needle, or an awl, from the hollow space to the outside; these will let air and water vapor escape as the piece is being fired, and prevent an explosion. If you make the holes in inconspicuous spots, they won't spoil the appearance of the work. (On a head, for example, a hole pierced inside an ear, or between parted lips, would scarcely be noticeable.)

Family. Coil-built. 16″ high, and glazed.

Figure by Arthur Freeman, 14″ high, carved from a solid block, fired and glazed. Note that, with a thick base like this, the base must be hollowed out before firing, to avoid cracking.

Figure by Arthur Freeman, 14″ high, carved from a solid block, fired and glazed. The base of this piece, too, was hollowed out before firing.

Coil-Formed Sculpture

After getting some experience with one or both of the previous methods, you may like to try sculpture by coil forming; this produces a hollow figure without the use of an armature, or without scooping out the inside.

UNFIRED POTTERY

Here's a way of treating greenware without firing. The method is not suitable for use with tableware, vases that are to hold water, or anything that is going to receive rough treatment; nothing replaces firing for such purposes. But for such things as wall plaques, sculpture, mobiles, necklaces, etc., it produces long-lasting, good-looking work. It's particularly suitable for use by children—or by grown-ups, for that matter, who want to spare the expense of commercial firing, or of buying their own kilns.

Dry the pot as usual, just as if you were going to fire it. When it is thoroughly dry, paint it all over with a mixture of 1 part white resin glue to 1 part water. Cover it completely, base and all. Stand it up on a 3-pointed stilt to dry, if you have one; if not, let the top of the pot dry, then lay it on its side, or turn it upside-down, and apply the mixture separately to the base. Drying of this first coat usually takes about 2 hours.

When it's quite hard, give a second coat all over, this time with undiluted glue. By the time this second coat dries, the pot will have a slight gloss. If you want a higher gloss, give it a third coat. This treatment seals the pores of the pot and gives it a tough surface.

Unfired Color

The glue layer formed like this is transparent, and will reveal the natural color of your clay, whatever it is.

If you want a colored effect, first paint the fully-dried pot with exterior latex paint—either one color all over, or in a multi-colored design of your choice. Let the paint get thoroughly dry *before* you begin to apply the glue. For some projects, such as sculpture and jewelry, you could apply antiquing over the paint, before adding the glue.

Figure and head by Edith Freeman. The woman is 10¾" and the head 8" high, realistic in proportion but without detailed features. They are unfired, finished with the paint and glue technique, and mounted on wooden bases. A head this size should be hollowed out; before finishing the top, scoop out inside with a spoon. Then, when the head is leather-hard, scoop out the inside of the neck.

THE TURNTABLE

Many potters find a turntable a useful piece of equipment. I should point out that the turntable is not the same thing as a potter's wheel; it is not built the same way, and does not serve the same purpose. You can buy a turntable quite cheaply at any good ceramic-supply store.

Incised Decoration

Suppose you have a leather-hard pot ready for decorating with an incised pattern. The turntable offers you an easy way to carve horizontal lines. Center the pot on the turntable and fix it in place with four lumps of damp clay stuck to the turntable. (Remove and store them after you've finished.)

Take the cutting-tool in one hand and press it against the pot at the desired height. (Put a block of wood, a brick, or something of the kind, under your wrist to keep the hand steady, if you like.)

With the other hand, turn the turntable. Presto! The tool cuts a perfect circle right around the pot. If need be, to get the desired depth of cut, take several turns, removing a little more clay each time.

Engobe or Glaze Application

Similarly the turntable offers a quick, accurate way to apply engobe or glaze to a pot in horizontal circles. Have the engobe or glaze on a brush; apply it to the pot at the proper level, then turn the turntable.

Circles of wax-resist can be applied in exactly the same way. Then cover the whole pot with engobe, fire it, and the pattern is revealed.

Still another method: paint the pot all over with engobe, then use the turntable to produce sgraffito circles as elements of the sgraffito design.

Coil and Strip Forming

Here's a way to facilitate coil or strip forming. Make the base for your pot in the usual way. Center it on the turntable. Prepare the first section of coil or strip. Apply one end of it to the edge of the base, then with one hand turn the turntable and with the other press the coil or strip into place as the base slowly rotates.

With a little practice, you should be able to produce well-shaped pots by this method. If there are any irregular spots, you can quickly restore a pot to roundness by paddling the sides while you turn it on the turntable. Or, if a pot has projections that stick out too far, hold a spatula in one hand, turn the turntable with the other, and cut off the projecting parts as the pot rotates.

Incising a line around a pot.

14

Back to Basics

WE'VE considered so far the buying of materials in ceramic supply stores, and firing in electrically-heated kilns; yet potters were at work long before such stores and kilns came into being.

Many people will find extra pleasure in going back to older, simpler ways of getting clay and firing pots.

DIGGING CLAY

Clay is to be found in city and country alike. Look wherever you see earth being excavated—for houses, apartments, stores, factories, highways —or where natural forces have laid bare the subsoil—in lake and river banks, cliffs, landslips, etc. Natural clay may be white, gray, brown, red or black.

Field Testing
It's no use wasting time and effort to collect clay that will be useless for your pottery. There are a couple of simple tests you can make outdoors, with just a small sample, that will give you a fair idea of the quality of the clay.

Equipment for prospecting trips: a garden trowel, a quart bottle of water, a few fluid ounces of 10 percent hydrochloric acid (from the drug-store), a medicine dropper, a few paper towels, and a few plastic bags.

Test for plasticity.

Dig up an egg-sized piece of clay. If necessary, add water, a little at a time, to make it soft enough for testing. (Or, if it's already too wet, use towels to absorb excess water.) Then roll the lump between your hands. If it crumbles to pieces, despite addition of extra water, it is no good for your purpose. If it is excessively sticky, clings to your hands, and won't let itself be molded into shape, it is no good. But if you can roll it out into a smooth cigar or cylinder, without crumbling, and without excessive sticking, then it shows promise.

Test for carbonates.

Clay that contains large amounts of carbonates may appear to be satisfactory for forming, but it probably will not fire well. So, with the medicine dropper, put a few drops of the 10 percent hydrochloric acid on your test piece of clay. If there is a vigorous bubbling and frothing, the clay contains too much carbonate, and is useless. A very slight bubbling is not objectionable.

Home Testing

If a sample of clay passes both field tests, put a few pounds of it in a plastic bag and, if necessary, attach a label showing exactly where you found it. Then take it home.

Pick out any foreign material—twigs, leaves, stones—cut the sample into pieces and thoroughly dry them.

Crush the dried clay into small pieces and pass it through a kitchen sieve, which will hold back any remaining foreign matter. Reconstitute the dried, broken clay as described in Chapter 3.

Then try the clay on whatever processes you wish to use, preferably making several small pots by different methods. See if the clay dries properly without cracking. See how it reacts to firing. See how it takes various decorative processes—staining, waxing, glazing, etc.

Digging in Quantity

In most locations, you can't just dig up clay in large quantities and cart it away! It's essential to find out who owns the land, and get permission; be prepared to pay something for the privilege, if necessary.

You'll need a pick and shovel, and some containers to carry the clay: 5-gallon drums, cartons, sacks, or heavy plastic bags are all handy.

Though you get the least possible amount of foreign matter with the clay, some cleaning process will probably be necessary. Separate the clay into small lumps and dry it thoroughly; then crack them into fingernail-size pieces and make them into slip, using 2 parts water to 1 part clay by volume.

Pass the slip through a kitchen strainer to remove the coarser impurities; then pass it through the 80-gauge sieve. Let the slip settle overnight, and next morning pour the water off the top. Pour a blob of the remaining slip on to a plaster bat; the excess water is quickly absorbed, and you are left with a lump of clay in workable condition. Take this lump off.

Repeat the process as often as is necessary (using a fresh plaster bat whenever the former one gets waterlogged) till you have treated the whole batch of clay.

FIRING WITHOUT A KILN

Here are three simple firing methods that require no special apparatus. It must be admitted that these methods do not give such close temperature control as will a kiln and pyrometric cones; yet, if you use clay with a fairly wide vitrification range, you should have no trouble on that score for biscuit firing. However, I would not recommend using these methods for glaze firing.

One advantage of using an actual fire is that the somewhat irregular heating of the pot, and the random movement of smoke, fumes and ashes may produce unusual effects of coloring that you could not have planned in advance.

The Fire-Pit

This method can be used if you have some place where you can dig a small pit in the ground, and a supply of firewood.

Make the pit about 18 inches square and 18 inches deep. In the bottom of the pit put a 6″ layer of sand, gravel or old bricks—something that will hold the heat. On this, stand the pots to be fired.

Now you don't want to build the fire right on and around the pots; so get a piece of iron grating like a fireplace grate, or a piece of heavy-gauge metal lath, or some iron bars. This iron is to go just above your pots, supported on bricks, rocks, cans full of sand, or anything that will hold it up and not collapse in the heat.

Now start a wood fire on top of the grate. Get it burning brightly and keep adding more wood. Fairly small pieces, well dried, are best, so that you get a clear, hot fire. Big, heavy chunks of wood might knock down the grate and bring the whole thing crashing down on to your pots.

Keep the fire burning brightly for 6 to 8 hours. By this time, a lot of small burning pieces will have fallen through the grate, so that the whole pit is full of glowing coals.

Now cover up the pit with dry sand or earth to keep the heat in, and leave it undisturbed overnight. Just as with a kiln, there must be no sudden cooling of the pots. Next day, strip off the covering, scoop out the ashes, and you should find your pots perfectly fired.

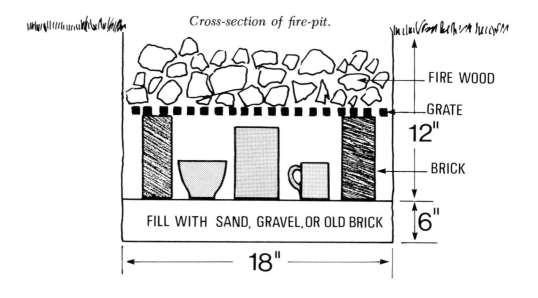

Cross-section of fire-pit.

FIRE WOOD

GRATE

12″

BRICK

FILL WITH SAND, GRAVEL, OR OLD BRICK

6″

18″

FIRE WOOD

CLAY FLOWER POTS

Firing in fireplace under flowerpot saggars.

The Fireplace

If you are going to have a good fire burning in your fireplace for several hours, you can take advantage of it to fire a few not-too-large pots.

Before lighting the fire, put your greenware in the fireplace and cover it with one or more clay flowerpots turned upside-down. (A pot thus used to protect greenware in firing is called a saggar.) Build your fire and keep it going in the usual way. Next morning, the pots should be properly fired.

The Barbecue

You can also fire in a charcoal barbecue. Cover the greenware with flower-pot saggars; build a good charcoal fire around and over the saggars; keep it going for 6 to 8 hours, then leave it overnight to cool.

Record-Keeping

With these methods, as with a kiln, you'll get best value from your materials and time by keeping written records. Indicate the kind and quantity of fuel used, the time the fire was kept burning, and any note-worthy details about the arrangement of the greenware, plus a summary of the results obtained.

GLOSSARY

Antiquing: highlighting raised parts of a design with metal.

Armature: temporary support for sculpture while shaping; removed before firing.

Ball clay: gray clay, very plastic; seldom used alone, but usually blended.

Bat: small board used to support a pot during working and drying.

Biscuit firing: the first firing; removes combined water, and usually produces a porous pot.

Bisque firing: same as biscuit firing.

Brick clay: produces red, porous pottery.

China clay: produces white pottery; needs high firing temperature.

Combined water: water chemically combined with clay; removable only by firing.

Cone pat: small lump of clay in which pyrometric cones are mounted for firing.

Cutting wire: wire used for cutting lumps of moist clay.

Crazing: cracking of glaze caused by unequal shrinkage of glaze and clay body after firing.

Dry-footing: leaving all or part of the base of a pot unglazed.

Engobe: clay mixture that, on firing, produces surface coloration on pots.

Egyptian paste: clay mixture that forms colored glaze in one firing.

Fettling tool: knife for cutting and shaping clay.

Firing: the heating process that turns clay into pottery.

Frit: fine-ground glass, used as an ingredient of glaze.

Glaze: a glass-like coating on the surface of pottery; often colored.

Glaze firing: second firing of a pot to produce a glazed finish.

Greenware: unfired pottery.

Grog: clay fired, then crushed to powder; often mixed with clay to improve its working qualities.

Grout: thin cement for filling joints between tiles.

Incising: cutting into a clay surface to produce a pattern in relief.

Kanthal: metal used for making kiln heating elements.

Kaolin: same as China clay.

Leather hard: clay that feels cool and slightly damp, but firm to the touch and hard enough to hold its shape; still soft enough to carve.

Mechanical water: water that makes clay soft for working; removable by air drying.

Modeling clay: mixed with grog; suitable for off-wheel working.

Nichrome: heat-resistant wire used for supporting clay articles while being fired.

Paddle: wooden strip used for shaping soft clay.

Pin: same as stilt.

Plaster bat: small slab of plaster of Paris used for drying too-wet clay.

Pyrometric cone: clay cone that melts at a specified temperature.

Sanding: procedure used after the final stage of drying to remove roughness, to correct shape, etc.

Saggar (or seggar): clay cover used to protect pots when firing in an actual fire.

Sculpture clay: same as Modeling clay.

Sgraffito: scratching through engobe to reveal the color of the clay beneath.

Slip: glue-like mixture of clay and water.

Slip coloring: same as Engobe.

Stilt: 3-pointed support of refractory material used in firing to hold a pot off the kiln bottom.

Stoneware clay: contains feldspar; needs high firing temperature.

Template: a pattern or gauge, usually of thin wood or cardboard, used as a guide in shaping a pot.

Terra Cotta clay: same as Modeling clay.

Vitrification: partial melting of clay in firing.

Vitrification range: temperature range between start of vitrification and complete melting.

Water of plasticity: same as Mechanical water.

Wedging: a process for uniformly distributing water, and removing air, in clay before working.

Wedging wire: same as Cutting wire:

SUPPLIERS OF POTTERY MATERIALS AND EQUIPMENT

U.S.A.

American Art Clay Co., 4717 W. 16th Street, Indianapolis, Indiana, 46222

Alaska Mud Puddle, 9034 Hartzell Road, Anchorage, Alaska, 99502

Capital Ceramics Inc., 2174 S. Main Street, Salt Lake City, Utah, 84115

Central New York Ceramic Supply, 213-215 Second Street, Liverpool, New York, 13088

Ceramics, Hawaii Ltd., 629 Cooke Street, Honolulu, Hawaii, 96813

Cross Creek Ceramics, 3596 Brownsville Road, Pittsburgh, Pennsylvania 15227

C. R. Hill Company, 2724-11 Mi. Road, At Coolidge Berkley, 48226

Sax Arts and Crafts, 207 N. Milwaukee Street, Milwaukee, Wisconsin, 53202

Standard Ceramic Supply Co., Box 4435, Pittsburgh, Pennsylvania, 15205

Tepping Studio Supply Co., 3003 Salem Avenue, Dayton, Ohio, 45406

Terra Ceramics, 3035 Koapako Street, Honolulu, Hawaii, 96819

Trinity Ceramic Supply, Inc., 9016 Diplomacy Road, Dallas, Texas, 75235

Van Howe Ceramic of Albuquerque, Inc., 4810 Pan American Freeway, N.E., Albuquerque, New Mexico, 87107

Western Ceramics Supply Co., 1601 Howard Street, San Francisco, Calif., 94102

Canada

Advance Ceramics, 820 Renfrew Street, Vancouver, B. C., V5K 4B6

Alberta Ceramic Supplies, 8520 67th Avenue, Edmonton, Alberta, T6E 0M8

Ceramicraft Ltd., 594 Notre Dame Avenue, Winnipeg, Manitoba, R3B 1S7

Coast Ceramics Ltd., 3739 West 16th Avenue, Vancouver, B. C., V6R 3C5

Cobequid Ceramics, 102 Smith Avenue, Truro, Nova Scotia, B2N 1C4

Pottery Supply House, 491 Wildwood Drive, Oakville, Ontario, L6K 1V1

Universal Ceramics, 623 8th Avenue, S. W., Calgary, Alberta, T2P 1H1

Village Ceramic Studio, 4949 Dundas Street, West Islington, Ontario, M9A 1B6

Australia

Ceramic Supply Co., 61 Lakemba Street, Belmore, N. S. W. 2192
Chullora Potteries (Pty.) Ltd., Waterloo Road, Greenacre, N. S. W. 2190
Ferro Corporation Australia Pty. Ltd., 16 Bermill Street, Rockdale, N. S. W. 2216
Thermic Appliances Pty. Ltd., (Kilns), 42 Parkes Street, Manly Vale, N.S.W. 2093

Denmark

M. O. Knudsens Eftf., Skallagardsvej 10, 4700 Naestved
Lyngbyovnen, Rypevang 6, 3450 Allerod

Norway

N. W. Damm & Son A/S, O. Slottsgate 6, Oslo 1
Hobbyhuset Global, N-4000 Stavanger
Harald Lyche & Co. A/S, 3000 Drammen
L. W. Tornoe A/S, N-5000 Bergen

Sweden

Cellbes Postorder AB, S. Strandgatan 20, S-503 30 BORAS
Ellos Postorder AB, S-501 86 BORAS
Josefsson i Boras AB, S-501 88 BORAS
Rowells Postordervaruhus, S-501 89 BORAS

United Kingdom

Harrison & Mayer Ltd., (Craft & Education Div.) Meir, Stoke-on-Trent, ST3 7PX
Fulham Pottery Ltd., 210 New Kings Road, London, SW6 4NY
Firogas Kilns Ltd., Sneyd St. Burslem, Stoke-on-Trent, ST6 2NT
The Diamond Clay Co., Ltd., Diamond Works, Hartshill, Stoke-on-Trent, Staffs
Sykes & Dyson Ltd., Queens Mill Road, Huddersfield, HD4 6AD

WEIGHTS AND MEASURES

The following conversion tables will be useful if you want to order from, or compare prices with, suppliers using a different system from your own.

Weights

(Metric equivalents correct to nearest 1/10 gram.)

¼ oz.	=	7.1 grams
½ oz.	=	14.2 grams
¾ oz.	=	21.3 grams
1 oz.	=	28.4 grams
2 oz.	=	56.7 grams
3 oz.	=	85.1 grams
¼ lb.	=	113.4 grams
½ lb.	=	226.8 grams
1 lb.	=	453.6 grams
2 lbs.	=	907.2 grams
5 lbs.	=	2.268 kilograms

1 gram	=	0.035 oz.
10 grams	=	0.35 oz.
50 grams	=	1.75 oz.
100 grams	=	3.5 oz.
250 grams	=	8.81 oz.
500 grams	=	17.64 oz.
1 kilogram	=	2.205 oz.

FLUID MEASURE

Although U.S. fluid measure uses the same names—fluid ounce, pint, quart, etc.—as British Imperial Fluid measure (used in Canada and the United Kingdom), the actual values of the units differ significantly; so here are two separate sets of conversion tables.

U.S. to Metric

1 teaspoon = 1/6 fl. ozs. = 5 milliliters
1 tablespoon = ½ fl. oz. = 15 milliliters
1 fl. oz. = 29.5 ml.
4 fl. ozs. = 118 ml.
1 cup = 8 fl. ozs. = 237 ml.
12 fl. ozs. = 354 ml.
1 pint = 16 fl. ozs. = 473 ml.
1 quart = 946 ml.

Metric to U.S.

1 milliliter = 1 cubic centimeter = 1/5 teaspoon
5 milliliters = 1 teaspoon
10 milliliters = 2 teaspoons
1 deciliter = 100 milliliters = 3.4 fl. ozs.
1 liter = 33.82 fl. ozs. = 1.057 quart

Imperial to Metric

1 teaspoon = 1/6 fl. ozs. = 5 milliliters*
1 tablespoon = ½ fl. oz. = 10 milliliters*
1 fl. oz. = 28 ml.
5 fl. ozs. = 142 ml.
10 fl. ozs. = 284 ml.
15 fl. ozs. = 426 ml.
20 fl. ozs. = 1 pint = 568 ml.
1 quart = 1.136 liter

Metric to Imperial

1 milliliter = 1 cubic centimeter = ⅕ teaspoon
5 ml. = 1 teaspoon
10 ml. = 2 teaspoons
1 deciliter = 100 ml. = 3.5 fl. ozs.
1 liter = 35 fl. ozs. = 1.75 pint

---

* The difference between U.S. and Imperial systems is not large enough to affect teaspoon measurements; it becomes significant when larger quantities are used.

Index